Adobe
Creative 3D
Workflows

A Designer's Guide to Adobe Substance 3D
and Adobe Creative Cloud Integration

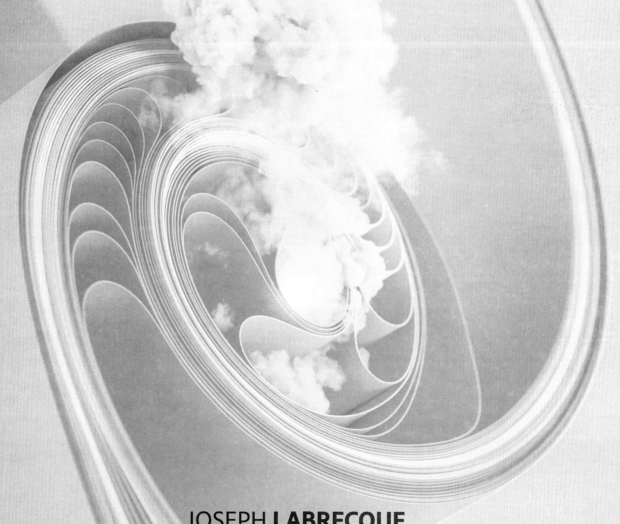

JOSEPH LABRECQUE

Adobe Creative 3D Workflows:
A Designer's Guide to Adobe Substance 3D and Adobe Creative Cloud Integration

Joseph Labrecque

Adobe Press
peachpit.com/adobepress

Adobe Press is an imprint of Pearson Education, Inc.
To report errors, please send a note to errata@peachpit.com

Figure Credits: Chapter 8, Empty guest room: jantsarik/Shutterstock; Chapter 8, A 360 degrees view of village: Simone Padovani/Shutterstock; Chapter 8, NASA's "Blue Marble 2002" composite: The National Aeronautics and Space Administration (NASA); Chapter 9, Graveyard_ pathways and Rainforest_trail: HDRI-HAVEN

Executive Editor: Laura Norman
Development Editor: Robyn G. Thomas
Senior Production Editor: Tracey Croom
Copy Editor: Scout Festa
Compositor: Kim Scott, Bumpy Design
Proofreader: Kim Wimpsett
Indexer: Rachel Kuhn
Cover Design: Chuti Prasertsith
Cover Illustration: Vladimir Petkovic
Interior Design: Kim Scott, Bumpy Design

ISBN-13: 978-0-13-828017-8
ISBN-10:   0-13-828017-7

1 2024

About the Author

Joseph Labrecque is a creative developer, designer, and educator with nearly two decades of experience creating expressive web, desktop, and mobile solutions. He joined the University of Colorado Boulder's College of Media, Communication and Information as faculty within the Department of Advertising, Public Relations and Media Design in autumn 2019. His teaching focuses on creative software, digital workflows, user interaction, and design principles and concepts. Before joining the faculty at CU Boulder, he was an adjunct faculty member at the University of Denver as well as a senior interactive-software engineer, user interface developer, and digital media designer.

Labrecque has authored several books and video course publications on design and development technologies, tools, and concepts through publishers such as Adobe Press, Peachpit, LinkedIn Learning, Apress, and Packt. He has spoken at large design and technology conferences, such as Adobe MAX, and for a variety of smaller creative communities. He is also the founder of Fractured Vision Media, LLC—a digital media production studio and distribution vehicle for a variety of creative works.

Joseph is an Adobe Education Leader, Adobe Community Expert, and member of Adobe Partners by Design. He holds a bachelor's degree in communication from Worcester State University and a master's degree in digital media studies from the University of Denver.

Acknowledgments

Putting together a book like this is an incredibly time-consuming endeavor. While certain people bear the brunt of the creative energy in a project like this, the team of others supporting and actively working to ensure that the project achieves its goals and the successes that come from those achievements is massive. Thank you to everyone who has had a hand in making this book a reality. Thanks to you as well, reader, for your trust in what we've put together here! I do hope you enjoy this work and benefit from it. The book contains an exciting set of topics for me, and I hope you can share in this enthusiasm.

Thanks to Laura Norman for her initial inquiries around the subject matter presented in this work and the subsequent support for what I've eventually brought into existence through this process. I also thank Robyn Thomas and Rob de Winter for their assistance and feedback during the writing and editing process. Their insights and recommendations have been invaluable in shaping the content and flow of the chapters within to be approachable and meaningful for you, the reader.

Also, I'm quite grateful to the people at Adobe from whom I have received assistance in the planning and resource-gathering phases of this project, especially Rebecca Hare, John Nack, and Michael Tanzillo. Thank you all.

Of course…as always…abundant love and appreciation to Leslie, Paige, and Lily.

—Joseph Labrecque

Contents

Introduction

Adobe Creative 3D Workflows: A Designer's Guide to Substance 3D and Creative Cloud Integration has a strange origin that actually has little to do with what it has become nearly a full year later.

In early 2023, Adobe released the first beta of its integrated set of generative AI technologies, named Firefly. This new artificial intelligence service was exciting, as it clearly stood out from existing text-to-image AI services. How so? Adobe expressed interest in integrating Firefly into a wide array of existing software applications. Moving beyond familiar text-to-image workflows could greatly augment the design capabilities of creative individuals through the use of AI across a variety of media.

Initially, a few additional integrations and expansions existed in preview—labeled as *In Exploration*—that were unlike anything I'd seen before when exploring generative AI software. In particular was a Firefly module given the name 3D to Image. The idea being that you could arrange a set of 3D models within the software, provide a descriptive prompt, and have Firefly generate a visual design based on the prompt and strongly influenced by the 3D models assembled across the canvas to form the resultant image.

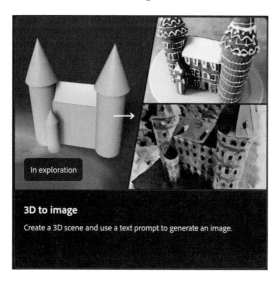

Although an exciting prospect for sure, that is not exactly what this book is about!

However, my interest in this 3D to Image module has, in a roundabout way, led to the book you are now reading. Discussions were begun around whether a book on Firefly generative AI—focused upon these 3D-focused aspects—would be a viable work. These discussions evolved into a different but related approach, as Adobe was also working steadily on integrating more traditional design software like Adobe Photoshop, Adobe Illustrator, and Adobe After Effects with capabilities and features derived from various Substance 3D collection applications and file formats—a melding of the worlds of 2D and 3D design software.

The result of all these discussions and initiatives is *Adobe Creative 3D Workflows*.

Who This Book Is For

The focus of this work is the integration that now exists across these different software applications and collections. Adobe Creative Cloud users who want to expand their design skills in the area of 3D will find this book useful. In a similar fashion, Substance 3D users who want an approach to using Creative Cloud software can find similar inroads, albeit from the opposite direction. In a general way, anyone interested in the intersections of 2D design software and 3D design software will benefit from exploring this work.

Considering the genesis of this work, I have been sure to integrate Firefly generative AI into the mix, as this service holds great promise in the creative space between 2D and 3D design. Adobe is taking wildly variant approaches to generative AI through its Sensei and Firefly models, and I am very excited to see how these explorations will impact 2D and 3D workflows in the coming years. Combine that with the expansion of the design techniques covered in this book and we have amazing opportunities to expand creativity ahead of us.

Whether your interest is in expanding traditional 2D-design workflows to include 3D components or you are coming from a 3D-tooling background to explore how these capabilities are being infused into 2D design software, I hope you find this book useful in combining these varied application workflows to create some truly fantastic results!

The Design of This Book

This book dives into the capabilities and workflows across the Adobe Creative Cloud and Adobe Substance 3D collections of design software. The focus is on the intersections between 2D and 3D workflows and how best to approach them when designing content with various techniques. This is an increasingly popular focus for Adobe and the wider design industry in general, and Adobe in particular has been bleeding these technologies together in meaningful and practical ways with increasing frequency and capability over the past few years.

Prerequisites

Before following the exercises in *Adobe Creative 3D Workflows*, make sure your system is set up correctly and that you've installed the required software and hardware. The system requirements for Adobe Creative Cloud and Adobe Substance 3D are here:

https://helpx.adobe.com/creative-cloud/system-requirements.html

You should have a working knowledge of your computer and operating system. For example, you should know how to use standard menus and commands and also how to open, save, and close files. If you need to review these techniques, see the documentation included with your macOS or Windows system.

It's not necessary to have a working knowledge of 3D design software concepts and terminology. Much of this will be explained in the first chapter. If you do come across a term that you're not familiar with, consult the glossary at the end of the book.

This is not an introductory book, however, and it is assumed you have some experience with Creative Cloud or similar software. For a comprehensive introduction to Adobe Creative Cloud design software, you should acquire a copy of *Adobe Creative Cloud Classroom in a Book* from Adobe Press, at *peachpit.com/ creativecloudCIB*.

Installing the Software

You must purchase an Adobe Creative Cloud subscription, or obtain a trial version, separately from this book. You can find help and resources at the following links for the software you will use in this book:

System requirements and complete instructions on installing the software: *helpx.adobe.com/support*.

Adobe Creative Cloud subscription: (required) This gives you access to Adobe's primary collection of software and includes applications like Photoshop, Illustrator, After Effects, and Animate—in addition to many other applications and services: *www.adobe.com/creativecloud*.

Adobe Substance 3D: (required) Adobe's collection of 3D-specific software is provided as a separate subscription and includes applications like Substance 3D Sampler, Substance 3D Stager, and additional applications meant for professional 3D work: *www.adobe.com/creativecloud/3d-ar.html*.

Complimentary Adobe Substance 3D subscription for higher education:
- If you are involved in higher education, you can acquire a complimentary subscription to Adobe Substance 3D by visiting *https://substance3d.adobe.com/ education/* and verifying your status.

- If you have a higher education enterprise account for Adobe Creative Cloud, the Substance 3D applications are often included with that subscription.

The first chapter in this book goes into everything you need to know when getting started with the software.

How to Approach the Chapters

The chapters in this book include step-by-step instructions. Some chapters are stand-alone, but most of them build on concepts and workflows from previous chapters. For this reason, the best way to learn from this book is to sequentially proceed through the chapters.

The chapters generally begin with an overview of a particular piece of design software and how to use it in the design of 3D content. They proceed by introducing concepts and workflows that are common to the individual workflows and applications involved until the project is complete. Often, content you design in a chapter will be used in a later chapter's projects to demonstrate the rich workflow you can achieve between these applications.

Many pages contain additional "sidebar" information boxes that explain a particular technology or offer alternative workflows. It's not necessary to read these additional boxes, or follow the workflows, but you may find them interesting and helpful, as they will deepen your understanding and often provide additional context. Tips and notes appear throughout the chapters and contain more situational, immediate items for you to apply during the current steps of a project.

By the end of the book, you'll have a good understanding of what each Adobe Creative Cloud or Substance 3D collection software application does, how to start a new project, and how to design useful content with the particular 3D workflows being explored.

Lesson Files

The projects in this book use supplied source files, including images, design assets, 3D models, materials, project files, and more. To complete the lessons in this book, copy all the files to your computer's storage drive.

The media files are practice files, provided for your personal, educational use in these lessons only. You are not authorized to use these files commercially or to publish, share, or distribute them in any form without written permission from Adobe Systems, Inc., and the individual copyright holders of the various items. Do not share projects created with these lesson files publicly. This includes, but is not limited to, distribution via social media or online video services including YouTube and Vimeo. A complete copyright statement is on the copyright page at the beginning of this book.

Any original media such as images, 3D models, materials, and so on that are referenced within or distributed as part of this book are copyright © 2024 by Joseph Labrecque. Certain additional design assets referenced are derived from direct use of online resources such as Adobe Express or as distributed within the software such as the case with Adobe Substance 3D Stager.

How to Access Online Material

You must register your purchase on *peachpit.com* to access the lesson files:

1. Go to *peachpit.com/3dworkflows*.

2. Sign in or create a new account.

3. Click **Submit**.

4. Click the **Access Bonus Content** link to download the bonus content from the Registered Products tab on your Account page.

If you purchased a digital product directly from *peachpit.com*, your product will already be registered.

Additional Resources

Adobe Creative 3D Workflows is not meant to replace documentation that comes with the software or to be a comprehensive reference for every feature. Only the commands and options used in the exercises are explained in this book. For comprehensive information about program features and tutorials, refer to the following resources.

Adobe Creative Cloud Learn and Support: *https://helpx.adobe.com/creative-cloud* is where you can find and browse Help and Support content on Adobe.com. On the Learn & Support page, click User Guide for documentation on individual features or visit *https://helpx.adobe.com/creative-cloud/user-guide.html*.

For inspiration, key techniques, cross-application workflows, and updates on new features, go to the Creative Cloud tutorials page at *helpx.adobe.com/creative-cloud/tutorials.html*.

Adobe Community: Tap into peer-to-peer discussions, questions, and answers on Adobe products at the Adobe Support Community page at *community.adobe.com*.

Adobe Creative Cloud Discover: This online resource offers thoughtful articles on design and design issues, a gallery showcasing the work of top-notch designers and artists, tutorials, and more. Check it out at *creativecloud.adobe.com/discover*.

Behance: Adobe's social network for creatives! Browse the work of others and get inspired through the sharing of creative design projects across traditional 2D design, 3D asset generation, and much more at *behance.net*.

Resources for educators: *adobe.com/education* and *edex.adobe.com* offer a treasure trove of information for instructors who teach classes on Adobe software. Find solutions for education at all levels, including free curricula that use an integrated approach to teaching Adobe software and that can be used to prepare for the Adobe Certified Professional exams.

CHAPTER 1

An Introduction to 3D Concepts

Welcome! This first chapter sets the stage for the concepts that follow and aims to provide you with a correct perspective and a solid foundation of knowledge that you can build upon as you discover specific software features and workflows across various 2D and 3D design applications. You'll learn the fundamentals of the software being used in this book, the approach to the exercises and workflows presented within, and most importantly the terminology, file types, and common considerations for working in 3D design software.

Because this book is written for more traditional Adobe Creative Cloud designers who want to explore additional 3D capabilities of the software they are already familiar with, it does not aim to be an introductory guide to applications like Adobe Photoshop or Adobe Illustrator. The assumption is that you already have the basics down and are comfortable with the applications.

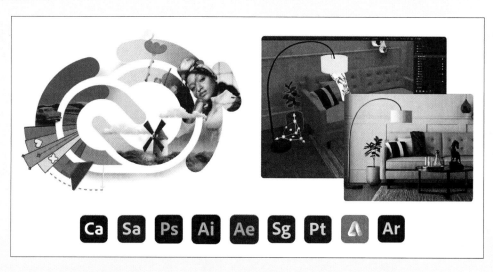

Applications that are part of Adobe Substance 3D are a different story. We will cover these in a more introductory manner while still ensuring that you can design usable assets and produce realistic 3D content.

NOTE If you would like a refresher of the basics of using software like Photoshop or Illustrator, have a look at *Adobe Creative Cloud Classroom in a Book: Design Software Foundations with Adobe Creative Cloud* (Adobe Press, 2022): *www.adobepress.com/store/adobe-creative-cloud-classroom-in-a-book-design-software-9780137914708*.

Our Approach to Designing in Three Dimensions

Before moving on to the more technical foundations of 3D file types and terminology, let's ensure clarity around the approaches and use of the software you'll be dealing with across the nine chapters of this book.

A Unified Approach to 3D Explorations

This book is meant to be a resource for those who want to explore what Adobe Creative Cloud and the related Adobe Substance 3D applications have to offer. You will be exploring tools that are part of both subscriptions from a general designer's viewpoint.

Following Adobe's acquisition of Allegorithmic (developers of the original Substance tools) in 2019, activity has occurred on both the Creative Cloud and Substance 3D sides of the company. Adobe has spun off the Substance applications into their own subscription in the form of Adobe Substance 3D and has simultaneously worked to integrate Substance 3D technologies into their flagship 2D design tools within Creative Cloud.

As tools like Photoshop, Illustrator, and Adobe After Effects adopt 3D workflows and features that dovetail with Adobe Substance 3D, there is a greater desire on the part of traditional 2D designers to understand how to design using 3D tools. Opportunity exists for creativity that goes well beyond what had been available to Creative Cloud designers.

Within these chapters are projects that weave through a good number of the workflows that exist across this unified set of software.

Approaches to 3D in Design Software

Traditionally, there have been two different approaches to achieving 3D design in software. Both have their place in the world of design, although each also has a set of benefits and drawbacks in terms of complexity, realism, and overall appearance.

One method is to enable the transformation of 2D objects using a 3D perspective warp. Using this method, all objects remain 2D and are simply modified to appear as though they exist in a 3D environment through a shift in perspective. This is sometimes referred to as "cards in space" because none of the objects has any depth whatsoever and always exists as a flat plane. Many older applications of 3D design in existing tools in Adobe Creative Cloud use this method.

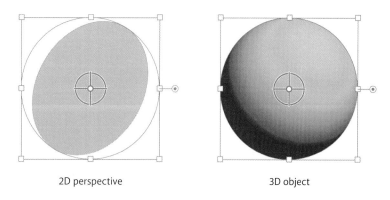

2D perspective   3D object

The second method involves the creation and use of actual 3D models within a design environment. This is a much truer version of 3D design and is the focus of this book. Many of the Substance 3D applications use only this method of 3D design.

Some of the applications that are part of Adobe Creative Cloud, such as Illustrator, After Effects, and even Adobe Animate, allow for both methods within the same software—which can have interesting results.

Adobe Substance 3D Software

Adobe Substance 3D is a separate subscription from Creative Cloud for most designers. Although the cost of maintaining two subscriptions may give you pause...Adobe maintains that there is a large enough division between Substance 3D and Creative Cloud users to warrant this split. For designers interested in using both collections of software, there really isn't much alternative.

NOTE Adobe Creative Cloud subscriptions at higher education institutions will often also grant access to Adobe Substance 3D. Additionally, if you are a higher education student or faculty, you may be able to use the collection for free. Visit *https://substance3d.adobe.com/education/* for more information.

The Substance 3D applications are installed and managed through the Creative Cloud desktop application, just like Photoshop, Illustrator, and other Creative Cloud software. You can locate these applications within the 3D and AR category along the left side of the Apps tab.

You will need the following Adobe Substance 3D software to complete the exercises in this book:

- **Substance 3D Sampler:** Transform your real-life pictures into 3D models, materials, and lights, and then mix and blend assets for even more advanced surfaces.

- **Substance 3D Stager:** Assemble and render photorealistic scenes. Use premade templates built by world-class photographers for stunning results in minutes.

- **Substance 3D Painter:** Turn any asset into a digital canvas. Paint detailed effects directly onto its surface with parametric brushes and smart materials.

NOTE We will review how to install applications from the Creative Cloud desktop application later in this chapter.

These three applications were chosen due to their familiar aspects with other design software and intersections across one another and other software as part of Creative Cloud. You will complete full, in-depth projects within each of these applications in the chapters that follow but will also explore additional Substance 3D applications and features in the final chapter of this book.

3D Capabilities within Adobe Creative Cloud Software

Although Adobe's 3D-focused efforts are aligned to Substance 3D, they've added 3D capabilities and integrations to their flagship Creative Cloud software over the past few years as well. Applications across both collections work incredibly well together and provide the sort of creative balance that this book addresses when designing 3D content.

As with Substance 3D software, you can access Creative Cloud applications via the Creative Cloud desktop application. Creative Cloud is not focused only on 3D, so you will find software to enable designs in photography, graphic design, audio, video, motion design, interactive, and more.

You will need the following Creative Cloud desktop software to complete the exercises in this book:

- **Adobe Animate:** You wil design interactive and animated virtual reality experiences for the web using time-tested motion and programmatic workflows.

- **Adobe Photoshop:** You will use Substance 3D materials within Photoshop to create realistic 3D effects earlier reserved for 3D native applications.

- **Adobe Illustrator:** You will create realistic 3D graphics by combining effects and lighting with materials sourced from Substance 3D.

- **Adobe After Effects:** 3D model import in After Effects allows you to import 3D models and render them in the same 3D space as native After Effects cameras, lights, and 3D layers.

These three applications were chosen due to their recent feature integrations with Substance 3D technologies and intersections with software as part of Adobe Substance 3D. Although this set of software is a focus of our in-depth explorations into 3D design, we will cover additional Creative Cloud applications and their implementation of 3D capabilities in the final chapter of this book.

NOTE Mobile apps cannot be installed directly from the Creative Cloud desktop app. See Chapter 2 for an overview of mobile app installation.

NOTE You'll need the Creative Cloud desktop application installed on your computer (macOS or Windows) to install most of the software you will be using in this book. Visit *www.adobe .com/creativecloud/ desktop-app.html* to download and install it.

You will also use the following mobile applications:

- **Adobe Capture:** With this application, you can generate realistic textures with rich 3D surface details.

- **Adobe Aero:** This application provides the most intuitive way to build, view, and share robust immersive storytelling experiences in mobile AR.

Desktop Applications—Install and Update

If you are a user of Adobe creative software, you'll already be familiar with the procedures for locating and installing applications on your macOS or Windows computer. For those of you who are completely new to this process—or could use a refresher—the following steps take you through the process of installing and updating individual applications using Creative Cloud desktop.

1. Browse the various categories within the Creative Cloud desktop app and locate an application you want to install.

    This example uses Substance 3D Sampler.

2. Select the application.

    A card element displays information about the application along with options to learn more about or install the specific piece of software.

3. Click the **Install** button to begin installation.

The Creative Cloud desktop application will begin downloading the most recent version of the chosen application from Adobe servers and begin installing it.

You can monitor the progress through a percentage-based loader while this process occurs.

If you change your mind at any time during the installation process, you can click the **Cancel** button to stop it.

Once the application you installed is ready, its appearance in the Creative Cloud desktop application changes, and the software can be launched by clicking the **Open** button.

You can also launch your installed applications in the usual way—per your chosen operating system options.

Since these applications are updated frequently, you should check for updates often.

4. Within the Creative Cloud desktop application, choose the **Updates** options from the Apps tab and click the **Check for Updates** button to see whether any of your installed applications have newer versions available.

The Creative Cloud desktop application will refresh and present all available updates to you in a list.

5. Click the **Update** button for any application you'd like to update to the newest version.

TIP Sometimes, updates include only performance enhancements and bug fixes, but often they also present new features for you to try. In either case, it is well worth your time to ensure you are using the latest versions of the software. Clicking the Enable Auto-update button in the Updates tab will ensure that your applications are always up to date.

When it comes to installing mobile apps, you can visit the app store for your chosen platform directly and search for the app by name.

Alternatively, you can send a link to your device to the app store directly from within the All apps > Mobile section of the Creative Cloud Desktop application.

You'll step through this process in detail at the beginning of the next chapter in order to install Adobe Capture.

Working with 3D Assets

As you begin exploring 3D design concepts, you will likely notice that terminology and common content types differ quite a bit from what you may be familiar with when using traditional design software. Of course, it's important to know at least a basic level what terms such as models, materials, and UVs refer to as you approach a 3D workflow, which will inevitably involve some or all these concepts.

Let's tackle some of the most common terminology in 3D design software first. We will focus on terms that are used heavily within the chapters ahead—though as you delve deeper into 3D design, you are likely to encounter many more.

Models

These are the 3D objects that are placed into scenes, have materials applied to them, and react to environmental lighting. When most people think of 3D design, this is what they envision, as models are the most tangible aspect to this sort of design work. By default, you will begin working with 3D models that have an untextured, white, plastic-like appearance. Depending on the type of model, textures may or may not be included.

Although simpler 3D models can be easily created using some of the software covered in this book, for anything approaching complexity you need a dedicated 3D modeling application.

Most models are composed of a series of interconnected polygons across a 3D mesh. The figure below is a 3D model of a deck chair.

It is structurally realistic, with a seat mesh and frame structures for the base and back, but the visual appearance is quite fake and plastic. This is because the default material applied to the model is meant to be simple and includes only the most basic of texturing properties.

Many 3D models can be acquired from a variety of online sources, and some of these are detailed in the next section.

Materials

Often referred to as textures, materials are representative of the appearance of real-world objects and are applied to 3D models to make them photographically realistic.

Much software, when presenting a basic, untextured model, will apply a plain default texture in order to render it with some visual form. Applying a photorealistic set of materials to any 3D model will enhance it so that it appears much more like fabric, wood, stone, or any other material that the object is composed of.

For instance, if you apply a blue nylon webbing material to the seat mesh of the deck chair model and then apply a stained wax patina wood texture to the deck chair frame base and back, its appearance becomes drastically more realistic.

No longer is the 3D model expressing a default appearance; rather, it is exhibiting details prescribed by the materials placed on the various objects that compose its structure. These materials also allow you, as the designer, to adjust various properties to dial in the exact look that you require.

UV Mapping

Another term you will encounter quite a bit when working with materials is *UV mapping*. UVs are related to materials in that they describe a coordinate system across both the U and V axes of a flat texture that determines how that specific texture should be placed to conform specifically to the 3D model. UVs are representations of a 3D model flattened into 2D space.

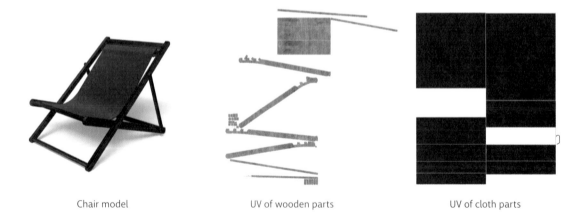

| Chair model | UV of wooden parts | UV of cloth parts |

This differs quite a bit from the application of general materials that can be placed across any 3D surface, as UVs are designed to align specifically with a certain 3D model. In this way, they are ideal for placing stickers, logos, damage, and rust across the surface of a model.

Lights

An often-overlooked part of the process, lighting can have a dramatic effect upon your textured models and make a massive impact on how realistic they appear. Hotspots, unlit areas, and the shadows cast by various objects are generated by the combination of the environmental and staged lights being used.

Let's take one last look at the deck chair model—this time being lit by an assortment of lights. The flat and uninteresting appearance of the textured model gains new life with the addition and placement of lights.

Lights, when placed poorly, can also impact the model's appearance—but negatively. Having too many or too few lights or positioning them too close or too far from a model can result in a poorly lit or overly lit appearance, and your scene will lose much of its realism. Lighting can be one of the trickiest aspects to get right when working in 3D design, so it is important to spend the necessary time adjusting your lights until you achieve the desired result.

NOTE Traditional lighting is something you must manually process yourself as you work with 3D objects. Some applications, however, will process lighting automatically for you based upon existing data. For instance, Adobe Substance 3D Stager can use artificial intelligence to determine the proper lighting of a scene based on environmental image data, and Adobe Aero lights 3D objects placed in augmented reality through lighting adjustments derived from real space.

Rendering

The act of rendering takes all these aspects into consideration when generating the visual representation of our 3D content. The models themselves, the materials applied to them, and the lighting being used are factors that determine how your design appears when rendered. In general, most 3D software uses some sort of real-time rendering while you are actively designing the 3D content and then makes use of a more intensive—and more realistic—rendering process when producing the final output. You can often switch to these additional rendering techniques during author-time to get a better idea of how lighting and shadows play across the design.

Ray Tracing

You will see the term *ray tracing* come up a lot when working in 3D design software. Most applications use real-time rendering by default because it is a quick way to achieve a somewhat realistic render as you work. Ray tracing is an alternative technique that shoots light rays throughout the scene, which the light bounces off of. The 3D objects and applied materials mimic what happens with actual cameras. This is a much more demanding process for your computer, but you can achieve much more realistic shadows, reflections, and translucency in your design.

Physically Based Rendering (PBR)

PBR provides a more accurate representation of how light interacts with material properties through shading and rendering. The idea behind PBR is that it describes the physical nature of the materials being represented so that lighting can be applied in a realistic and accurate way under any lighting condition. For instance, a material that is more translucent in reality allows more light to pass through it within its 3D representation. Materials that allow no light to pass though their form—such as concrete or stone—behave as expected as well. All of this works together to form a realistic representation of how objects react to light from each light source, and the light bounces across and passes through nearby objects. This form of rendering is used in all Substance materials.

Mixed Reality

Mixed reality (XR) spaces are a unique set of environments within which to express your 3D designs in interactive space. 3D objects that you design in certain software can be employed within these environments as true 3D objects or as renderings—depending on the environment and technologies being employed. Let's look at the two most popular forms of mixed reality through augmented reality and virtual reality examples.

Augmented Reality (AR)

When working in augmented reality, you rely on an actual, physical environment for the placement of your 3D objects. The "augmented" layer of content exists upon the "reality" layer, which is the true physical space as seen by the camera. Augmented reality can use specialized and expensive hardware or, more commonly, the camera of a common mobile phone for the user to view and interact with the scene.

For example, in the figure below, you can see the deck chair in augmented reality, courtesy of an Apple iPhone and the Adobe Aero mobile application.

This technology is used in an increasing number of ways in both the creative and retail spaces. Many online retailers, for example, now include an option to view furniture or other objects in your home through augmented reality prior to purchase. As for more creative uses, experimental digital sculptors employ augmented reality to place their works in the environment of an exhibit or gallery alongside other artists.

NOTE We will explore how to create an augmented reality scene for Adobe Aero in detail in Chapter 7.

Virtual Reality (VR)

Another application of mixed reality technologies is virtual reality. This is an older form of mixed reality that differs from augmented reality in that all aspects of "reality" are truly "virtual." Your 3D models—or even just renderings of them—are placed in a virtual environment. The user can often look around the environment and interact with objects in it.

In this figure, the deck chair is in a fantastic virtual environment composed of a beach with a looming castle across the waters. This is obviously a virtual environment, but the deck chair can be placed within it just as it can within augmented reality.

NOTE We will have a quick look at how to create a virtual reality scene using Adobe Animate in Chapter 10.

Given that virtual reality has been around for quite some time now, there are many implementations of this type of mixed reality environment across all sorts of devices and platforms. In the example given here, we are using a browser-based virtual reality platform provided by Adobe Animate software.

3D File Types to Know

When exploring 3D design software for the first time, you will likely encounter file formats that are completely new to you. We'll examine some of these file types in more detail as they are encountered in subsequent chapters, but for now, let's look at some of the most common file types and what they are used for.

- **OBJ:** This is a very common 3D object file type that can be used in just about any 3D design software. Basically, this is the closest thing to a universal 3D format.

- **FBX:** This is a more advanced 3D object file type that can also contain animation data alongside advanced materials, cameras, and lighting. It is commonly used in gaming and mixed reality applications.

- **GLTF:** This file type has capabilities similar to those of an FBX file but is open source (FBX is proprietary). Due to its open nature, it is often used as a 3D file format on the web. (GLB is a binary version of GLTF.)

- **USD/USDA/USDZ:** Developed by Pixar, USD (Universal Scene Description) is typically used to store entire scenes' data. The format was expanded on in recent years by Apple and Pixar, specifically for use in 3D augmented reality applications through the USDZ sub-format.

- **MDL:** This is an Adobe Standard material and a subset of the NVIDIA Material Definition Language. These are more basic material types available in some software.

- **SBSAR:** This is a Substance material as developed by Allegorithmic, the precursor to Adobe Substance 3D. These are more advanced materials that can exhibit many custom tweakable properties, a set of explicit presets, and more. Most of the software covered in this book uses this material type.

- **REAL:** This is an Adobe Aero project file that can be shared with other designers as a unique project.

Of course, many other file types are in use across the wide array of 3D design software that exists. This small sampling includes some of those that you will encounter as you work through this book and the various workflows you explore in the chapters to come.

Resources for Acquiring 3D Assets

While we will go through a number of ways to create your own assets—both models and materials—in the following chapters, there are a lot of resources to know about that provide a large number of quality, ready-made assets for your use in 3D design software.

Starter Assets

As you move through the applications and workflows in this book, you will notice that many of them—across both Creative Cloud and Substance 3D—include a set of ready-to-use starter assets.

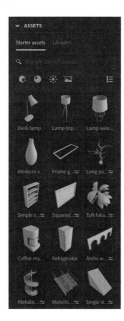

Photoshop, Illustrator, and Substance 3D Stager, as well as other Adobe applications, contain assets to get you started working in 3D design. These assets can often be filtered by model, material, and light, depending on the application and workflow being used.

Starter assets can get you working in 3D space quickly and easily without having to leave the application you are designing with.

Adobe Stock

Another good resource for assets is Adobe Stock. It contains all sorts of useful content for photography, illustration, video content, and more. There is also a pretty good set of 3D assets to discover here.

1. Visit *https://stock.adobe.com/search/free* in your web browser of choice.

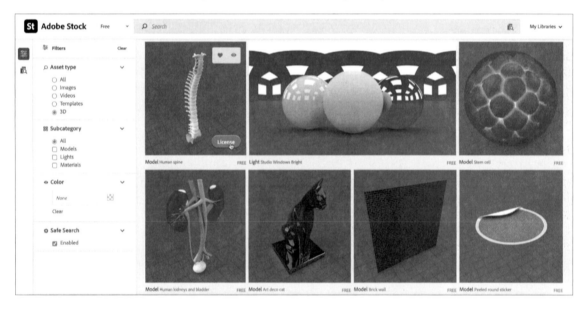

You may need to sign in with your Adobe ID, but once that is complete, you will have access to the free Adobe Stock library.

In the Filters sidebar, you can filter by asset type.

2. Choose **3D** from the **Asset Type** list.

This selection presents all the free 3D models, materials, and environmental lights that you can access through this resource.

Remember that Adobe Stock is not only for stock photos but can be used to gather all sorts of content.

NOTE While you have accessed the Adobe Stock free library here, you can access the full 3D assets library by visiting *https://stock .adobe.com/search/ 3d-assets*. Many of these assets, however, are not free.

Substance 3D Assets

One of the best resources from which to gather 3D assets is Substance 3D itself. As you may imagine, assets that are part of the collection are very high quality and cover a massive number of potential uses across various industries. They can all be accessed from a web browser or from within the Creative Cloud desktop application.

Keep in mind that Substance 3D Assets library content must be purchased using available credits ![1271]. Most subscribers to Adobe Substance 3D get 50 credits every month, but this will vary by subscription plan.

Let's explore how to access Substance 3D assets from within a web browser.

1. Using a web browser, visit *https://substance3d.adobe.com/assets*.

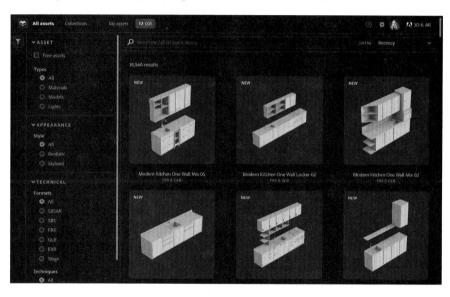

You may need to sign in with your Adobe ID, but once that is complete, you will have access to the Substance 3D Assets library.

From here, you can filter assets by type, style, format, and more by making choices along the left sidebar.

2. If the Filter options are not open for you, click the **Filter toggle** ![icon] to open the sidebar.

Once you find an asset you'd like to use, you can download it to your computer.

3. Hover over the asset preview until the **download button** ![icon] appears and click the button to download the asset.

The Substance 3D Assets library includes several asset collections, which are curated sets of models, materials, and more.

TIP To explore Substance 3D assets from within the Creative Cloud desktop application, switch to the Stock & Marketplace tab and choose 3D from the horizontal list of asset types at the top of the screen.

TIP You can also search assets by using keywords and search terms from the search input at the top of the interface. Search terms and filters can be used together to refine your search.

4. Click the Collections tab at the top of the interface to access the asset collections.

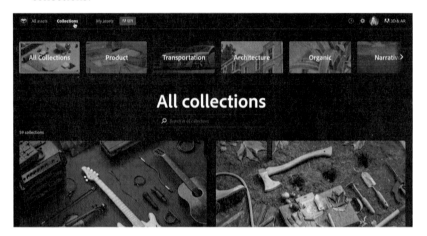

Various collections appear, and you can browse the assets grouped within. You can also search the collections for something specific by using the search input.

Earlier, you saw how to download an asset by clicking the download button that appears on the preview when you use your mouse to hover over it. If you want more detail, click any asset to view a larger representation of it.

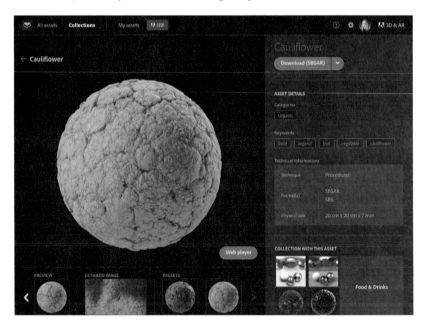

You will also be able to view asset details and download the asset from this detail view.

Substance 3D Community Assets

Alongside the Adobe-curated Substance 3D Assets library is a related resource of community-submitted content available in Substance 3D Community Assets. The main difference between the two collections is that the Substance 3D Community Assets library content is free to download.

To visit the library, enter *https://substance3d.adobe.com/community-assets* into your web browser of choice and begin browsing.

Similar to what you have seen with Substance 3D Assets library, you can use the categories to filter content and enter search terms to locate exactly what you want within the collection.

Clicking any submission in this collection will bring up a detailed view that allows you to view asset details and download counts and see what software applications are compatible with the chosen asset. Of course, you can also download the asset for use in your own 3D design projects by clicking the large Download button on this screen.

NOTE You can also be a contributor to the Substance 3D Community Assets library if you have designed materials, models, or other assets for use in 3D design. Once you have created assets through explorations in this book, you may want to consider sharing them through this resource. In Chapter 10, we'll explore exactly how to do that!

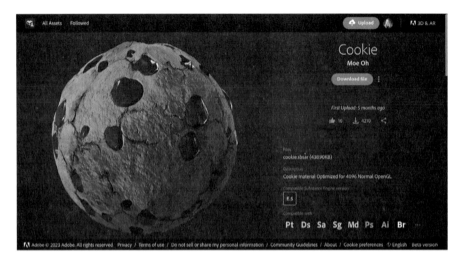

Once downloaded, the asset file can be freely used in any design project within the listed compatible software applications.

Additional Considerations

Here's a quick overview of concepts that will come up often in this book in the use of the application menu, cameras, and gizmos.

Navigating Software Application Menus

You will find many commands and suggestions outlined in the project steps across the chapters that follow. Many of these have to do with identifying and accessing the application menu. Application menu structure is dictated by the underlying operating system, and there are small differences in how they appear on macOS versus Windows.

Adobe Photoshop application menu on macOS

Adobe Photoshop application menu on Windows

These important menus appear at the very top of the screen on macOS and on the application frame on Windows. As you can see in the figure, the same menu options exist on both operating systems, as only their display and layout differ.

If you are not already acquainted with them, I suggest launching a couple of the applications and inspecting their application menu locations—in particular, where to access the File menu option. Document and project creation, the saving of files, and even exporting and publishing are often done from the File option in the application menu, regardless of your operating system.

Common 3D Tools and Concepts

Whether you're using 3D tools and workflows in dedicated 3D software applications or in traditional 2D design software, there are a couple of tools and concepts they share.

Cameras

The camera and the tools that control camera views are mentioned in some projects in this book. In 3D design software, you can generally manipulate the position, rotation, and scale of individual objects. Within some of these applications, you will also have a camera available to adjust the view of all objects at once by framing the scene.

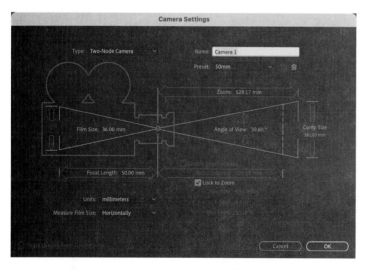

Some software, such as After Effects, allows you to control cameras through tweaking specific properties—like focus and aperture—along with positioning and transformative properties. Other software—such as Substance 3D Stager—enables the adjustment of property values such as depth of field while manipulating camera dolly, pan, and orbit settings through specific camera tools available from the application toolbar.

No matter how a camera is manipulated in a piece of software, the general idea is the same. The camera determines the framing and view of all aspects of your document or project. Camera properties can be manipulated to adjust the overall design of your 3D composition.

Gizmos

Individual objects in a document or scene can be manipulated by changing the values associated with properties such as position, scale, and rotation. This can often be done using a unified properties panel with a specific object selected, but most 3D design software provides the same control through an interactive overlay referred to as a *gizmo.*

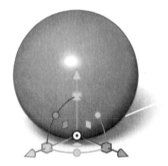 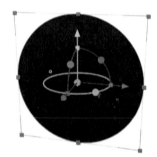 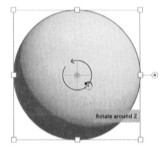

A gizmo generally appears once an object has been selected and often exhibits different colors for each of the 3D axes you can manipulate—x, y, and z. In addition, the various shapes and spines that make up the gizmo's form represent properties such as position, scale, and rotation along each of these axes.

You'll encounter gizmos a lot in the chapters to come. Knowing what they are used for and knowing that their appearance may differ depending on the software being used are good bits of information to hold onto.

Let's Go!

All right—let's move ahead to Chapter 2 and start designing with Adobe 3D creative workflows! Each chapter that follows is dedicated to a certain workflow and focus on a single design software application, but many chapters also branch out to use additional software to enhance results.

By the conclusion of this book, you'll be comfortable using 3D design tools across Creative Cloud and Substance 3D, and you'll be able to explore advanced tools and workflows comfortably.

NOTE If you have not already downloaded the project files to your computer from your Account page on *peachpit.com,* make sure to do so now. See the "Getting Started" section at the beginning of the book.

CHAPTER 2

Generating Custom 3D Materials

With terminology and the various types of 3D assets and file formats covered in the previous chapter, we'll now examine how to use different software to generate sets of assets for use in 3D applications, with a focus on designing materials. The primary tools you will use to produce materials in this chapter are Adobe Capture and Adobe Substance 3D Sampler.

Adobe provides several tools that produce materials that can be used across a variety of additional applications. Materials can be used in Adobe Photoshop, Illustrator, Substance 3D Stager, and more.

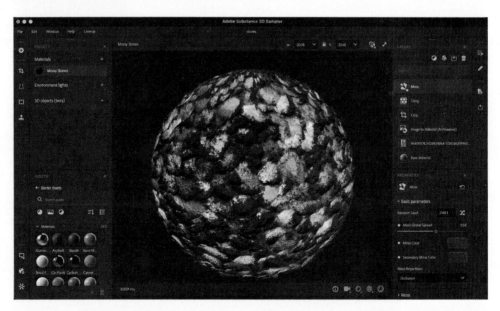

We'll explore the primary methods for designers to create materials using Adobe Creative Cloud tools and Adobe Substance 3D.

Generating Basic Materials
with Adobe Capture

Adobe Capture is a mobile application that can be installed on either Apple iOS or Google Android. Although certain user interface elements and capabilities will differ between these two platforms, the major features of Capture remain identical across both.

Installing Adobe Capture

Adobe Capture runs on mobile, so the installation isn't as straightforward as the installation of the software that runs on the desktop, as you must install it from the official app store for either mobile platform.

The most guided method of installing Capture is through the Creative Cloud desktop application.

1. With the Creative Cloud desktop application installed and launched on either macOS or Windows, choose **Apps** from the top navigation and **All apps** from the side navigation.

    You are taken to the All Apps view, which contains tabs along the top for Desktop, Mobile, and Web.

2. Switch to the Mobile tab by clicking it, and scroll down until you locate the card for Capture. Click the **Send Link** button.

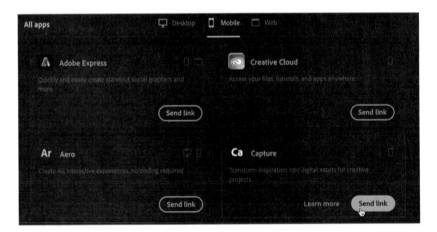

    The **Send Capture link** overlay appears.

3. Within the **Send Capture link** overlay, choose whether you would like to receive a link to install the app via **SMS** or **Email** and enter the required personal information.

4. Click the **Send Link** button.

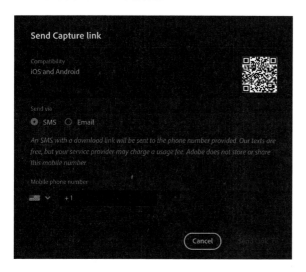

5. Check your device text messages or email (depending on which method you chose) to receive a direct link to your platform's app store for installation.

Once the app is downloaded and installed, you can launch it by tapping the Capture App icon.

With Capture launched, you will find yourself at the Libraries view, which displays any Creative Cloud Libraries you have created. If you have never used Libraries before, you will see only a default library named *Your Library*.

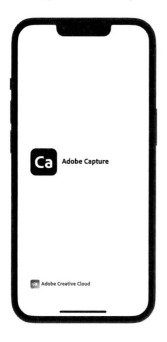

NOTE You can always install Adobe Capture by visiting the app store directly for your device platform.

NOTE Libraries are managed collections of design assets that you are able to organize across work environments and even share with others. Learn more about the benefits and use of Creative Cloud Libraries at *https://helpx.adobe. com/creative-cloud/ help/libraries.html.*

Some additional controls are also accessible from within this view, including a tabbed navigation bar at the bottom that allows easy access to Create, Learn, and Discover content.

- **Libraries:** This provides access to your Creative Cloud Libraries and any content within each.

- **Create:** This brings you to a screen where you can choose what sort of content you'd like to capture. You'll explore this view in depth as we proceed.

- **Learn:** You can access tutorials that walk you through the various features of Adobe Capture.

- **Discover:** Access featured projects on Behance, "the world's largest creative network for showcasing and discovering creative work."

NOTE Placement and location of these various controls and navigation items may differ depending on the platform you are using.

You will also find floating controls along the side of this view for capturing audio with the device microphone, capturing image-based content through the camera, and importing images and audio files for content generation.

Creative Cloud Libraries are integral to using Adobe Capture—as any content that is created with this app will be placed into a library for easy access within traditional desktop software.

Capturing Materials

Let's go ahead and use Adobe Capture to create a material for use in 3D workflows by sampling from the surrounding environment.

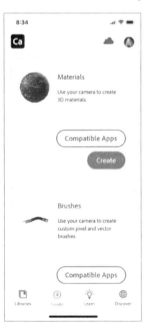

1. From within the Libraries view, tap **Create** ⊕ to begin the capture process.

   A series of cards describing the different types of assets you can generate appears.

2. Scroll down through the set of cards to locate the **Materials** card and tap the **Create** button.

   You could also tap the **Compatible Apps** button to see a list of applications that can use materials generated with Capture.

3. Once the camera view appears, locate an interesting bit of wall or floor texture around your location to base your new material on.

   Because you entered the camera mode by clicking the **Materials** card, Materials mode is automatically selected. You can swipe left or right above the shutter release to switch capture modes, but for this exercise, stick with Materials, of course.

4. Take a photo by tapping the **Shutter Release** button  at the bottom of the screen.

Once the photograph is taken, you are brought into the edit workspace. Here, you can switch between the Refine and Crop views.

5. Make any adjustments you feel would benefit the generation of your material.

A preview is included in the Refine view so that you can see immediate results from your choices when releasing these sliders. You can also use your finger to move the preview around—viewing all sides of the rendered object with the material applied.

At the bottom of the Refine view is a set of sliders to adjust properties like roughness, intensity, metallic, detail, and more. You can even change the shape of your 3D object from the default spherical preview to a cylinder, cube, and more by clicking any of the icons along the bottom.

The Crop view allows you to focus on a particular area of your image to be used for material generation.

Do not tap the toggle switch **Convert to AI powered material** just yet. You will examine this feature later in this chapter.

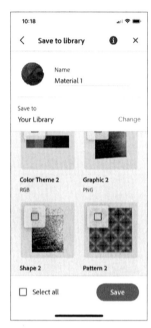

6. Once you are happy with your adjustments, tap the **Save** button.

   You are taken to the Save to Library view, where you have a chance to rename the material and select which library to save it to.

   Below this is a set of additional content types that can be generated from your captured image, such as color themes, patterns, graphics, shapes, gradients, and more.

7. Tap the **Change** link next to **Save to** to choose a different library to save your material to.

   The Choose Library view will appear and list all your existing Creative Cloud Libraries.

8. Tap the **Plus** button ＋ to add a new library, and enter **Materials** for its name within the overlay that appears. Tap the **Create** button to create the new Materials library.

The overlay disappears, and the new Materials library is selected.

9. Tap the **Name** field, rename the material **Flooring**, and tap the **Save** button to save your Flooring material to the Materials library.

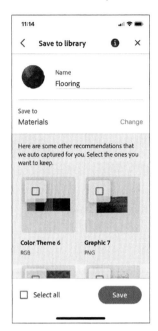

The Flooring material has now been captured, refined, and saved to a library named *Materials*.

You can continue to capture new materials from any objects or textures around you for use in various workflows. Creative Cloud Libraries sync across mobile, web, and desktop—allowing you to easily use this new material in any supported applications.

Creating AI-Powered Materials

Along with the standard material type you just created, Adobe Substance 3D subscribers can use AI to enhance their materials to include additional qualities such as surface texture and displacement effects.

Let's copy your existing material and convert it through artificial intelligence to express these advanced qualities.

1. Navigate to the Libraries view by tapping the **Libraries** icon ▢ within Adobe Capture.

   The Libraries view lists all your Creative Cloud Libraries for easy access.

2. Tap the Materials library that you created in the previous section.

   This library contains the Flooring material you created earlier.

3. Tap the small ellipse icon ••• below the Flooring material thumbnail preview to open a menu of additional options for the material.

 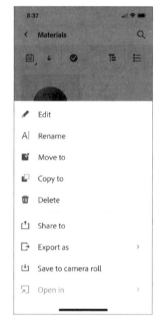

4. From the overlay menu that appears, choose the **Copy to** option.

   This provides the ability to make a copy of your material—either within the same library or in a different one.

5. In the Copy to view that appears, tap the library itself to create a duplicate within that library. In this case, you tap **Materials**.

The Copy to view closes, and you return to the chosen library. Both the original material and the duplicate are present.

Next, you will now edit one of the materials to change it to an AI-powered material.

6. Tap the small ellipse icon ••• to open a menu of additional options for the material.

7. Select the **Edit** option.

   It doesn't matter which one you edit, as they are identical at this point.

8. Tap the **Convert to AI powered material** toggle switch to activate it.

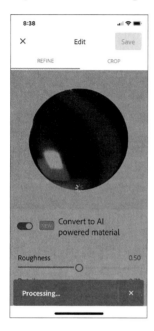

The material is sent to the Adobe Sensei AI and processed into a more advanced type of material. The new AI-powered material is then downloaded and replaces the original.

9. Tap the **Save** button to complete this conversion process.

   Although the thumbnail previews for each material look quite distinct from one another, you likely will want to rename your AI-powered material as well.

10. Tap the ellipse icon ••• to reveal the material options menu and tap the **Rename** option.

11. Rename the AI-powered material **Flooring - AI**.

    Renaming will help you better distinguish between the original and the AI-powered duplicate.

You now have two distinct materials in your library based upon the same captured sample. The new, AI-powered material includes advanced qualities such as displacement, which is apparent by viewing the differences in height across the surface of the material within its thumbnail preview.

Using Materials from Capture

Even though the AI-powered material is more advanced than the original, basic form, it isn't perfect. Seams are likely visible across the surface of the texture, and there may be other things you want to adjust to increase the realism of this material. This is where Substance 3D Sampler comes into play in an Adobe Capture workflow when creating custom materials.

You can easily send an AI-powered material to Substance 3D Sampler for refinements and finishing.

1. Within the Materials library, tap the AI-powered duplicate material to enter Preview mode.

   Within Preview mode, several options become accessible, such as **Edit**, **Share**, and, for AI-powered materials, an **Open In** option. Basic materials will not include this option.

2. Tap the **Open in** option to reveal the Open In overlay menu.

   The option to open the material within Substance 3D Sampler will be present.

3. Tap the **Substance 3D Sampler** option in the Open In menu to remotely launch Sampler and additionally send the chosen material to the software for further refinement.

You are now finished working with Adobe Capture. You can safely close this mobile app as you move to work with desktop software.

On the desktop, Substance 3D Sampler should have launched with the material from Adobe Capture loaded in as a new project. As you can see in the image, there are definitely adjustments that could be done to make this material more realistic—including the removal of sharp, unblended edges.

NOTE Are you unfamiliar with working in Sampler? No worries—you will explore working with Substance 3D Sampler in depth in the next section. You'll briefly adjust your material here first.

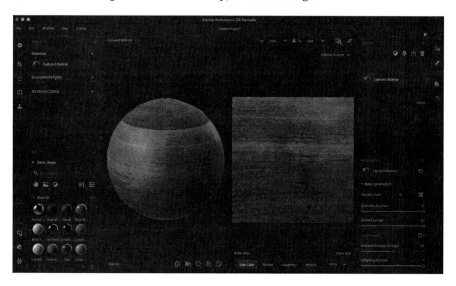

Adding layers such as *Make It Tile* and *Dirt* within the Substance 3D Sampler **Layers** panel can have a massive positive effect on any material created in Adobe Capture!

Let's perform some quick actions in Sampler that will demonstrate the power and ease the use of this software before moving on.

1. Locate the **Layers** panel in the upper right of the interface and click the **Add a Layer**  button.

   The Filters overlay appears and lists many, many filters.

2. In the search field above the list of filters, enter **make** and the **Make It Tile** filter appears. Click this filter to apply it to your material.

   The seams from the captured material edges should be much less noticeable and may actually disappear with just this single filter.

3. Click the **Add a Layer**  button once more from within the **Layers** panel to reveal the Filters overlay.

4. In the search field above the list of filters, enter "dirt" and the Dirt filter appears. Click this filter to apply it to your material.

With the Make It Tile and Dirt filters applied to the AI-powered material from Adobe Capture, you now have a pretty solid idea of what Substance 3D Sampler is capable of. The material is now seamless, with the texture being nicely tiled and a layer of dirt applied across it to cover any lingering imperfections.

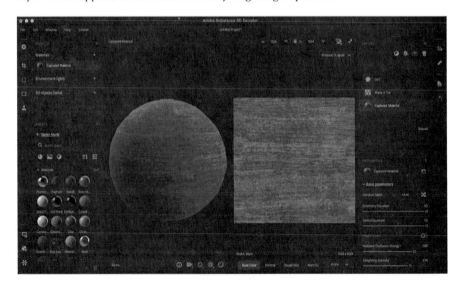

Your material from Adobe Capture looks much more realistic now! Let's continue to save your improved material and close the project.

5. Choose **File** > **Save As** from the application menu to open the Save dialog box.

6. Browse to the location you'd like to save your Sampler project to, provide a meaningful name for the file, and click **Save**.

   The project is saved, and the dialog box closes.

7. Choose **File** > **Open Home Screen** from the application menu to close the project and return to the home screen.

   This is where you will begin in the next section.

NOTE Your original material still exists within the Creative Cloud Library you saved it to through Adobe Capture. The Sampler version is unique to this software and does not write changes back to your original material.

This is just one workflow for creating a material using Adobe Capture and refining it within Substance 3D Sampler. It is also possible to create a new material from a simple photograph using Sampler. In the next section, you'll take an in-depth look at this very workflow.

Designing Advanced Materials with Substance 3D Sampler

Although using Adobe Capture is a mobile-focused method of creating materials, you can also create materials with desktop software from a photographic image by using Substance 3D Sampler. This is a very powerful method of creating advanced materials that provides many additional options compared to what you've seen in Capture.

Creating a New Project

When you first launch Substance 3D Sampler, you are presented with a home screen that is similar to what you may be used to when using software like Adobe Photoshop. You have the main area of the screen reserved for recent files, and a sidebar to the left with project-focused options such as **Create New** and **Open**.

You will start by creating a new file for your Substance 3D Sampler project.

1. With Sampler launched and the home screen visible, click the **Create New** button at the top of the left sidebar.

   A new project opens within Sampler.

2. Choose **File** > **Save as** from the application menu options at the top left of the interface.

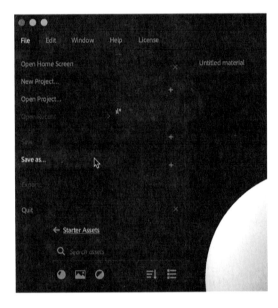

   A system-level Save dialog box appears.

3. Browse to the file system location you want to save your project file to and enter the name **stones** because you will be designing a mossy stones material from an existing photograph. Click the **Save** button.

   The project is saved to your local file system as a Substance 3D Sampler (*.ssa*) file.

You will be immediately taken to the Sampler project and can continue working within the interface.

With a new project established, you can now have a quick overview of the interface to locate various panels and options that you will use through the remainder of this chapter.

- **Project panel:** This displays the various types of assets you are working with in any particular project. These assets can include materials, environmental lights, or even 3D objects derived from a series of overlapping photos of a real-world object. Although our focus is on materials, Sampler is capable of much more.

NOTE The menu in Substance 3D Sampler is integrated within the application frame, whereas with most Adobe desktop software, you will find these options in the standard application menu.

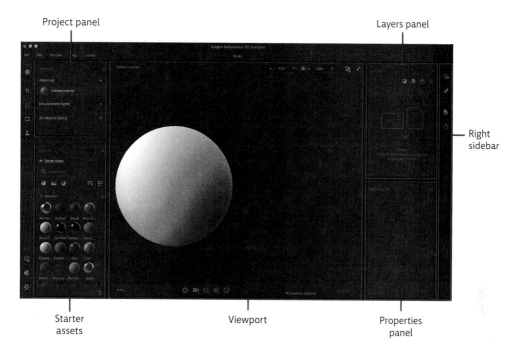

Project panel

Layers panel

Right sidebar

Starter assets

Viewport

Properties panel

- **Starter assets:** As with other Substance 3D applications, a set of starter assets is available for immediate use. These assets include materials, images, and filters.

- **Viewport:** The Viewport displays a basic 3D object that your material will be projected onto and also a flat representation of the material being worked on. These views are side by side by default, but the Viewport can be changed to display 3D or 2D view only as well.

- **Layers panel:** This is a representation of your project layer stack. Layers can consist of images, filters, materials, and more. These layer types all work together to establish your custom texture.

- **Properties panel:** This works in tandem with the **Layers** panel. With a layer selected, properties for that layer appear within the **Properties** panel and can be adjusted there to achieve your desired look.

- **Right sidebar:** This is where you can find collapsed versions of various panels such as **Metadata** and **Export**. You will be using the Export option to generate a custom material from your work in Sampler that can be used in other design software.

You will not be accessing all these interface elements within this project, but it is important to know what many of these elements are for, as they appear prominent within the interface as you work.

IMG_2703.JPG
JPEG image – 5.0 MB
Information   Show More
Created   Sunday, May 21, 2023 at 2:31 PM
Modified   Sunday, May 21, 2023 at 2:31 PM
Last opened   Tuesday, July 25, 2023 at 2:01 AM
Dimensions   2960×4032
Resolution   72×72

Importing a Photograph

Similarly to how you created a material with Adobe Capture, you will begin your exploration of Substance 3D Sampler with a captured photograph of a real-world object—in this case, a collection of small stones.

The photograph is part of the exercise files for this chapter and is named *IMG_2703.JPG*. It is straight out of the camera with no manipulation.

You can see that the lighting is rather uneven in the photograph, which would normally be a big problem when creating a seamless texture that tiles properly. As you'll soon see, this is not a problem for Sampler.

1. Either drag and drop the file into the **Layers** panel or click the prompt within the panel to locate the file.

    The Material Creation Template overlay appears. Within the overlay, **Image to Material** is selected automatically, and **AI Powered** is chosen as the method to use.

2. Click the **Import** button.

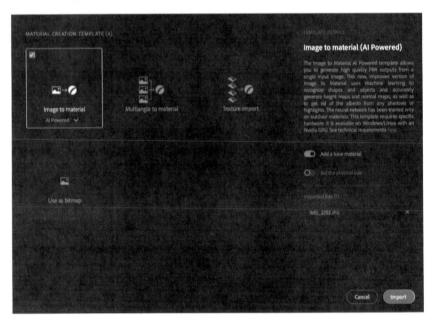

As with what you saw with material generation in Adobe Capture, you can choose whether you want to create an AI-powered material or use a B2M (bitmap to material) process. This can be switched from the small drop-down at the bottom of the **Image to Material** tile. B2M is the simpler bitmap-to-material approach, whereas AI Powered performs several additional processes upon the image being used.

The photograph will be processed by artificial intelligence mechanisms, and you will see an activity icon within the **Layers** panel indicating it is being processed. Once complete, the material will appear projected onto the model within the Viewport, and you can select the various layers in the **Layers** panel to view layer properties.

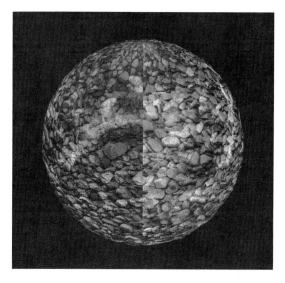 

While the AI process did a great job at representing height information for the stony texture, due to the uneven lighting and sharp edges of the original photograph, there are sharp boundaries where the texture repeats and wraps across the 3D model.

You can fix this using a variety of filter layers in the project.

Cropping and Tiling the Photographic Texture

Now, let's refine which portions of the photograph are best suited for the material and ensure that everything tiles so you can use your material across several different surfaces and it will still look good.

Nearly everything in Substance 3D Sampler can be achieved using various layers. You currently have a *Base Material* layer, the photographic layer, and the *AI Powered Image to Material* filter layer, which resides at the top of the layer stack.

NOTE Layers in Substance 3D Sampler are often much more like adjustment layers and filters in something like Adobe Photoshop. Generally, if you are adding a layer, you are adding some sort of process or effect to your base material.

You will first add a *Crop* filter layer to the project.

1. In the **Layers** panel, click the **Add a Layer**  to reveal the Filters overlay.

2. Scroll down to locate the **Crop** filter and click it to add a Crop filter layer to the top of the layer stack.

You could also activate the **Crop** tool in the left sidebar and a Crop filter layer will automatically be added to your layer stack.

The Crop filter has been added to the layer stack and is automatically selected.

TIP When layers are added to the layer stack, they always appear at the top of the stack. You can adjust this stacking order by dragging them up and down the layer stack.

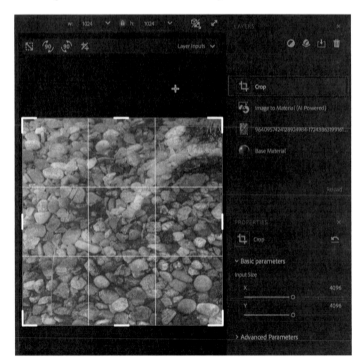

A crop frame appears in the 2D view that can be adjusted by dragging any of the side or corner handles. Not only will this adjust the crop in the 2D view, but the 3D view projection will update to match as well.

3. Adjust the Crop filter by adjusting the crop handle overlays to define a portion of the photographic image that does not include any major differences across the crop.

The edge seams will still be present when projected upon the 3D object, but your goal when cropping is to specify which portion of the original image you want to use in the projection. We'll address the tiling problem next.

4. In the **Layers** panel, locate the **Add a Layer**  button and click it to reveal the Filters overlay.

You have a lot of filters to choose from! You can also perform a search for a specific filter by entering a search term in the input at the top of the Filters overlay.

5. Scroll down or use the search input to locate the Tiling filter and click it to add a *Tiling* filter layer to the top of the layer stack.

The Tiling filter will likely do a good job at removing the straight and obvious seams from your texture. If you need to adjust it, though, that is where the **Properties** panel comes into play.

6. In the **Properties** panel, with the *Tiling* filter layer selected, activate the **Show Seam** toggle switch.

With the **Show Seam** toggle active, you can see the result of the Tiling filter upon both 2D and 3D projections of your texture.

As you can see from the image, the Tiling filter does a great job of minimizing or even removing the previously obvious seam from the texture. You can adjust both the Crop and Tiling properties to achieve an even more seamless flow across the projection.

Tiling vs. Make it Tile

Two primary filters are used to ensure your imagery tiles in a believable way across the projection without any hard edges or seams. The Tile filter and the Make it Tile filter are both used to achieve the same goal, but their implementation is slightly different.

- The Tile filter scales and offsets your material to generate an overlap, and then it varies the overlapping edge to hide the seam.

- The Make it Tile filter works by overlaying multiple copies of the material on top of one another.

For some materials, using the Tiling filter alone will still result in artifacts or problems along the seam. In this case it's a good idea to use other tools, such as Clone Stamp, to fix seam and tiling problems.

Working with Additional Filters

As mentioned, the layer stack in Substance 3D Sampler allows you to combine a variety of images, filters, and materials to produce your own unique textures. Although the Tiling filter you applied in the previous section can do a good job at blending the edges of your cropped image into one another when projected onto a surface, adding filters that simulate dirt, corrosion, or even moss can help really bind everything together while adding creative elements.

You'll now add some generated moss to your stone texture to complete this design.

1. In the **Layers** panel, click the **Add a Layer** button  to reveal the Filters overlay.

2. Locate and click the Moss filter to create a new Moss filter layer at the top of the layer stack.

   The Moss filter includes several default properties that are immediately applied to your existing projection.

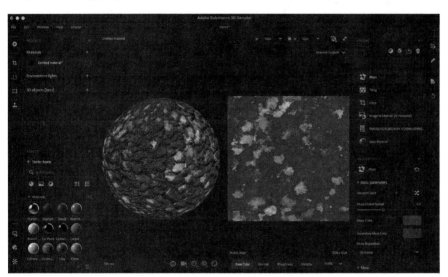

Because you are designing an advanced, AI-powered material, you have height information exposed via displacement properties. This information is determined by the AI based upon the original photographic imagery.

These default property values produce a thick moss that covers most of the surface. Let's make some adjustments to customize how this filter layer is applied to your texture.

3. Ensure the Moss filter layer is selected and look in the **Properties** panel to view the current Moss property values.

4. Make the following adjustments:

   - Moss Global Spread: **0.33**

   - Moss Color: **#2e3f0b**

   - Secondary Moss Color: **#4c180f**

The mossy texture takes on a darker and more complex appearance, and the amount of moss coverage is dialed back somewhat so that you can see more of the stony surface exposed.

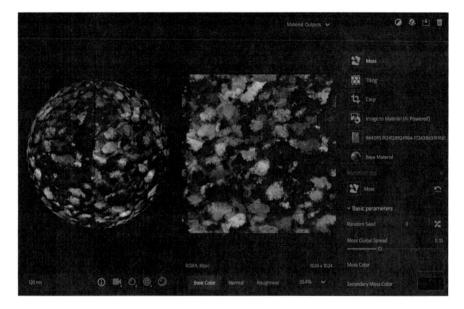

Not only does this look great, but it further obscures any problematic seams within the overall material projection.

Preparing Materials for Export

This material is now complete and ready to be exported. However, before doing so, there are some additional considerations that should be made.

If you or another designer will be using this material in other software (such as Stager, Painter, Photoshop, or Illustrator), you may want to be able to adjust the moss color or other filter layer properties there as well. By default, this isn't possible, but there is a solution for that: you can expose the various properties in the **Properties** panel so you can then easily manipulate them in other supported software.

1. In the **Properties** panel, hover over each of the three parameters that you previously adjusted—**Moss Global Spread, Moss Color**, and **Moss Secondary Color**—to locate the **Expose This Parameter** toggle  and click the toggle to expose it.

    A small teal circle appears to the left of the exposed property names.

Another step toward export preparation is to provide a meaningful name to the material you've designed.

2. In the **Project** panel, right-click your material, currently named *Untitled Material*, and choose **Rename** from the menu that appears.

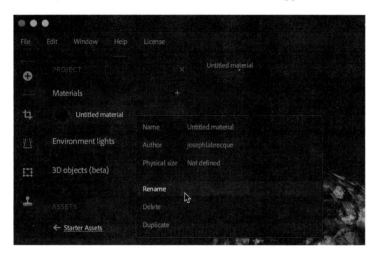

The name is now directly editable in the **Project** panel.

3. Type **mossy_stones** as your material name and press **Enter** on your keyboard to commit the change.

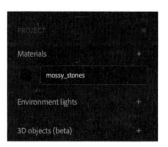

The name of the material in the **Project** panel updates to reflect the change.

With exposed properties chosen and a proper name given to your work, the material is ready for final export.

Exporting a Substance 3D Archive Material File

Although there are a number of advanced options and various share workflows from Substance 3D Sampler to other applications and file formats, you will perform a standard export and create a reusable Substance 3D Archive (*.sbsar*) file from your Sampler project.

1. Click the **Share** button ⬆️ in the right sidebar.

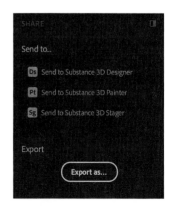

The Share overlay appears and contains options that allow you to send your material directly to other Substance 3D applications or to perform a standard export to file.

NOTE We'll look more deeply into Substance 3D Painter and Substance 3D Stager in Chapter 6 and will have an overview of Substance 3D Designer in Chapter 10.

2. Click **Export as** in the Share menu overlay.

3. In the **General Settings** section of the **Export as** overlay that appears, enter a name and location for your exported file. I suggest saving the file to the exercise folder you are currently working in.

4. Click the **Export** button to begin the export process.

You can explore the **Material Settings** section if you want, but for the purposes of this book, keep these settings at their defaults.

NOTE The Export Queue section appears only during an export.

It can take some time to perform the export, and you can actually queue up a number of exports to process one after the other. A progress bar appears in the Export Queue section of the Share overlay.

Once the export is complete, your distributable *.sbsar* file is in the location you previously chose.

You can use this file in many 3D software applications—and even some traditionally 2D applications like Adobe Photoshop or Illustrator. In the next few chapters, you'll explore some of the integrations between Substance 3D technologies (like *.sbsar* files) and traditional 2D design software.

CHAPTER 3

Applying 3D Materials to 2D Graphic Compositions

Often, the path of minimal confusion in adopting new workflows is to integrate these concepts into an area that you are more familiar with. Both Adobe Photoshop and Adobe Illustrator include features that intersect common 2D workflows with newer 3D concepts and tooling.

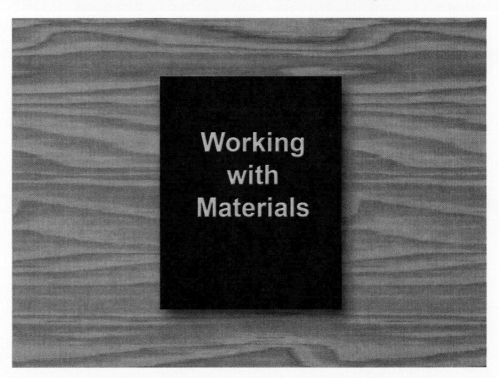

In this chapter, you will focus on applying 3D concepts upon 2D compositions within Photoshop.

3D Tools in Adobe Photoshop

Photoshop already has an interesting history when it comes to the integration of 3D within the software. In years past, designers had access to a full 3D workspace and several features that allowed the representation of 2D layers as 3D shapes via perspective warping and a set of text extrusion tools. However, in August 2021 Adobe announced that these workflows had been deprecated and that they would eventually be removed from Photoshop entirely.

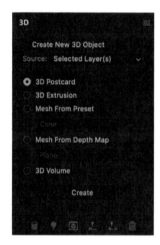

The reasons for this are twofold. For one, those older 3D workflows rely on out-of-date CPU and GPU technologies that operating systems have largely moved away from. Additionally, with the introduction of the Adobe Substance 3D, the focus is primarily on steering users toward these dedicated 3D applications to perform 3D work. That isn't entirely cut and dried, of course.

> With this transition to newer native APIs, together with the recent reboot of 3D tooling at Adobe featuring the Substance line of 3D products, the time has come to retire Photoshop's legacy 3D feature set and look to the future of how Photoshop and the Substance products will work together to bring the best of modern 2D and 3D to life across Adobe's products on the more stable native GPU APIs.
>
> —*Adobe*

Common Questions on Discontinued 3D Features

To read more about discontinued 3D features in Photoshop, visit the following resource: *https://helpx.adobe.com/photoshop/kb/3d-faq.html*.

Since deprecating the workflows, Adobe has been integrating certain subsets of Substance 3D technologies into Photoshop in ways that make the most sense for 2D designers. For instance, perhaps you need to add a texture to one of your layers in Photoshop as the background of an advertisement, poster, or some other composition. You could certainly get a stock image of the material you intend to use—but you are still at the mercy of the photographer as to whether the object matches what you imagine, whether the lighting is correct for your composition, and many related factors.

With the introduction of the **Materials** panel in Photoshop, the designer now has control over all these aspects of a composition.

The **Materials** panel can be accessed through the application menu by choosing **Window** > **Materials**. This panel allows access to modern 3D tooling within Photoshop and includes two tabs:

- **Materials:** This tab provides access to a set of materials that ship with Photoshop, and once a material has been applied, you can make adjustments to the various material properties.

- **Lighting:** Once a material has been applied, you can adjust how the lighting is applied through this tab.

We will be working with the **Materials** panel for the remainder of this chapter as we design a book cover and scenic background using a combination of Substance 3D materials and more traditional Photoshop workflows.

NOTE The Photoshop **Materials** panel currently supports only materials that are of the Substance 3D asset (*.sbsar*) file type.

Accessing Additional Materials

Although a good number of materials comes packaged within Photoshop, it is also possible to import your own materials or those that have been gathered from other sources.

- Click the **Add** button ➕ to browse for *.sbsar* files on your local computer.
- Click the Substance 3D **Assets** button 🎁 to search for *.sbsar* files from the Substance 3D website.
- Click the Substance 3D **Community Assets** button 🎁 to search for *.sbsar* files from the Substance 3D Community Assets website.

We examined several ways to acquire and create materials and other assets in Chapter 2.

Working with 3D Materials

To explore 3D materials in Photoshop, let's begin with a simple starter asset in the form of a Photoshop document file. There is nothing extraordinary about this file whatsoever—it exists only to provide a place to begin your work.

Open the file named *materials.psd* in Photoshop to begin.

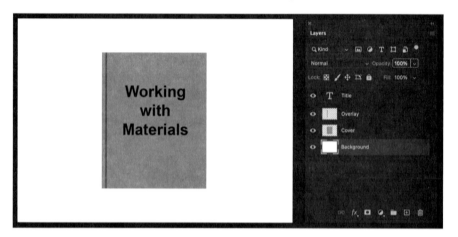

With the file opened within Photoshop, you can see the basic form of a book with the title "Working with Materials." The Photoshop starter file consists of a set of basic layers with a plain appearance. In examining the **Layers** panel, note there are currently four layers that make up this visual:

- **Title:** This is a text layer that makes up the book title—the typeface is Arial Bold, but you can always change it to something more interesting if you like. You will add a metallic material to the type layer.

- **Overlay:** This layer is simply a pixel layer used as an overlay to represent the crease made by the book's spine. It is black with a 30% Opacity value adjustment. You will not be applying a material to this layer—it exists only to define the book's spine.

- **Cover:** This layer is simply a rectangular set of pixels that represents the body of the book cover. You will add a fine leather material to this layer to make the book look realistic.

- **Background:** This is simply the background of the composition and is currently a set of white pixels that cover the entirety of the document. You will add a rough wooden material to this layer so that the book appears to have been placed upon a table or workbench of some sort.

The colors used for these layers exist only to keep everything visually distinct. As you add materials to each layer, it is the material that will be visible and not the actual pixel color values as they are displayed here.

Applying Materials to the Background

Let's deal with the *Background* layer first. It serves as the surface upon which the book will sit. You'll want to emulate something like a floor, tabletop, counter, workbench, or other such surface. Several materials are available that will serve this purpose.

Here is how to go about it:

1. Select the layer named *Background* from the **Layers** panel. If your Layers panel is not open, you can open it by choosing **Window** > **Layers** from the application menu.

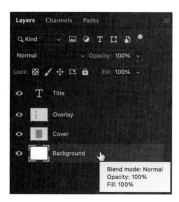

   Substance 3D materials are applied to layers in Photoshop, and you must ensure the correct layer is selected.

2. Open the **Materials** panel by choosing **Window** > **Materials** from the application menu.

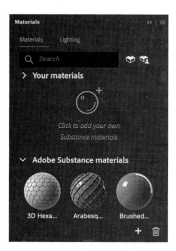

   A variety of built-in materials are available to you, or you can import your own materials for use in the composition.

3. Browse the list of materials and locate the material named *Natural Plywood*.

   Of course, you can also use the search text input to locate materials by name.

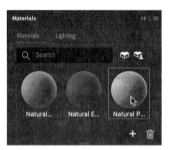

4. Click the chosen material to apply it to the selected layer.

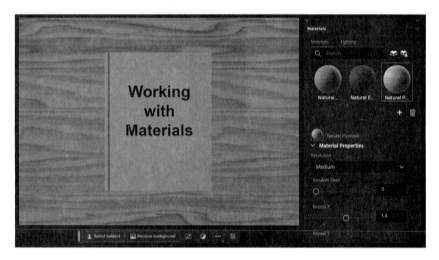

NOTE The new layer is transformed into a Smart Object; the material is applied via a Smart Filter and is named *Substance*.

The default properties for the chosen Substance 3D material are applied to a copy of the selected pixel layer (*Background*).

The original pixel layer remains unchanged, and the new layer appears above it in the stacking order. It is up to you to decide whether to hide or even delete the original layer.

5. In the **Materials** panel, beneath the materials selection section, locate the numerous Material Properties options that you can adjust for the Natural Plywood material you've selected.

I've set the **Resolution** value of my material to **High**, but you may want to leave it at the default choice, which is **Medium**. A **Resolution** value of **High** will look more detailed and realistic but will take additional resources to render.

Several properties, which are common to all materials and that you may want to adjust, are available in this section of the panel:

- **Random Seed:** When this is adjusted, it impacts the randomized aspects of some material properties. When attempting to replicate similar results across layers, you should use a specific value and repeat this value for each instance.

- **Repeat X/Repeat Y:** These refer to how the material is scaled as it is tiled across your layer. By default, the values are automatically configured based upon the ratio of your layer.

- **Repeat Uniformly:** This checkbox ensures that both X and Y repetitions scale evenly in reference to one another.

- **Repeat Uniform Scaler:** This slider increases or decreases the uniform scaling value.

- **Physically Sized:** This checkbox enforces the real-world, physical size of the chosen material. This is often not desirable in Photoshop, as it often makes the texture too large or too small—but is convenient for understanding the appropriate size that a material was designed for.

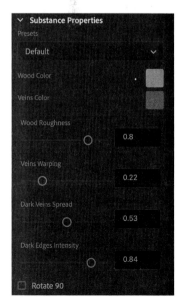

You'll now adjust the Substance properties to increase the realism of your Substance 3D material as applied to this layer within your composition.

6. Collapse the Material Properties section by clicking the Material Properties heading within the **Materials** panel and ensure the Substance Properties section is open and visible. These sections may also be collapsed and expanded by clicking the small chevron to the right of each section heading.

Substance Properties settings are generally both numerous and technical. Unlike the Material Properties settings, which are common to all materials, Substance Properties settings are specific to the chosen Substance material and are intentionally exposed as adjustable properties by the material designer.

Even though these properties change based upon the chosen material, there are some common ones:

- **Presets:** Many Substance materials have a set of baked-in presets that apply a certain look to your chosen material. The Natural Plywood example has presets for a **Default**, **Scratched**, and **Glossy** appearance. This works similarly to the presets found in an application like Adobe Photoshop Lightroom in that each preset automatically adjusts the various individual parameters to achieve a certain look that you can then continue to modify as you see fit.

- **Colors:** Often, any given material has more than one exposed color property. The Natural Plywood example has color values for wood, veins, and even scratches.

In addition to presets and color settings, you will likely have access to numerous properties specific to each material. The Natural Plywood example has properties such as the roughness of the wood, how dark veins appear, and even a subsection called *Wood Natural Filter* that contains additional controls for items like scratches and damage relief.

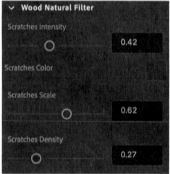

Let's continue working through the example and adjust a set of the exposed Substance materials for the Natural Plywood background layer.

7. In the Substance Materials section, adjust the **Wood Roughness** value to **0.8**.

8. Adjust the **Dark Veins Spread** value to **0.53**.

9. Within the **Wood Natural Filler** sub-section, adjust the **Scratches Intensity** value to **0.42**.

10. Change the **Scratches Color HEX** value to **3c250a**.

11. Set the **Scratches Scale** value to **0.62**.

12. Adjust the **Scratches Density** value to **0.27**.

You can see in comparison how these adjustments have affected the appearance of the Natural Plywood material.

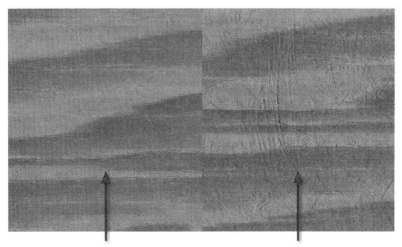

Original material properties | Adjusted material properties

Continue adjusting these properties if you would like to experiment with additional looks for your background.

Additional Materials Panel Sections

You also have access to additional sections for each material that are fairly uniform across all materials.

- **Position:** These values impact both the position and rotation of your material texture within the material itself.

- **Technical Parameters:** Luminosity, Contrast, and Saturation are parameters that are more photographic in nature and adjust the visual aspects just as an adjustment layer does in Photoshop—though there are also parameters here for aspects of a texture, such as the simulated height.

You may need to adjust these parameter values to dial in the exact look you are going for with a material or to assist in blending an applied material with the rest of your composition.

Applying Materials to the Book Cover

Now that you have chosen a material for the background and have a good grasp of how to use the **Materials** panel in Photoshop, let's turn our attention to the design of the book. You'll create the appearance of a leather-bound volume in this example.

1. Select the *Cover* layer so that it is highlighted as the active layer in the **Layers** panel.

2. Right-click (or Command/Ctrl-click) the layer thumbnail and choose **Select Pixels** from the menu that appears.

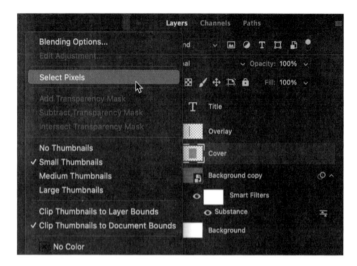

A selection appears on your document with the visual book selected.

You can apply Substance materials in Photoshop to full layers or selections. When no selection exists, the material replaces the layer. With an active selection in place and the material applied, the selection becomes a mask— taking the visual form of the selection.

3. In the **Materials** panel, search for the phrase *cowhide leather* and choose the Natural Cowhide Leather material from the results.

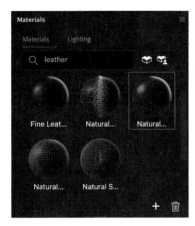

A new layer is created named *Cover copy* that includes a mask based upon the previous selection, and the Substance material is applied as a Smart Filter.

NOTE Smart Filters are filters that are applied to Smart Objects within your document. Smart Filters are "smart" in that they can be adjusted following their application, whereas regular filters cannot be.

The book cover takes on the appearance of leather.

4. In the **Materials** panel, look at the Substance Properties section and view the various properties that can be adjusted and are specific to this material.

This includes a list of diverse leather presets, the color to be used, the roughness, the grain scale, and even the wrinkle intensity for the leather material. You can choose to modify any of these properties as you want—but I am leaving them at their defaults for this object.

5. In the **Materials** panel, click the Lighting tab to display the Lighting properties.

The Lighting properties are the same for any material. They include a set of attributes that determine how the selected material is lit:

• **Rotation:** This value determines the horizontal angle of the light, with 0 degrees being the bottom of the document canvas.

  • **Height:** This value determines the vertical angle of the light, with 0 degrees being parallel to the surface of the document canvas.

  • **Color:** This value determines the color of the light, which can be adjusted with a color picker. The default color value is pure white.

  • **Exposure:** This value determines the power and intensity of the light.

  • **Displacement:** This value increases or decreases the difference between the highest and lowest points of the material.

TIP Adjusting any of these property values can have a dramatic effect upon the appearance of your material—so be careful!

NOTE Lighting will affect only the single object and material that is selected at the time. This differs from other software, such as Substance 3D Stager, where your lighting adjustments affect all objects in a composition simultaneously.

Applying Materials to Title Text

The Photoshop **Materials** panel is not confined to layers and selections. You can also apply materials to type layers.

Let's give the current type layer—representing the title of the book and part of the overall visual book cover—the appearance of precious metal. A golden, metallic look will go well with the rich leather cover you've already designed.

1. Select the existing type layer named *Title* in the **Layers** panel.

The type currently reads "Working with Materials" and is using 28pt Arial Bold with a color value of black.

2. With the type layer selected, open the **Materials** panel and locate the material named *Gold Leaf Fold*.

The default material preset is applied to your selected type. The type on the book cover now resembles metallic gold lettering.

As you've seen before when applying materials to layers and selections, a copy of the selected type layer is created.

However, note that this copy is set up as a clipping mask, and you can still adjust the type layer below to edit the type.

3. Within the Substance Properties section, select the **Fold Blur** preset and adjust the following values:

- Fold Variation: **0.5**
- Fold Blur: **0.6**
- Grain Intensity: **0.6**
- Roughness: **0.5**
- Metallic: **0.7**

NOTE Again, it is important to recall that every material has its own unique set of Substance properties that can be adjusted. You never really know what you'll encounter before applying a material and exploring!

These adjustments give the title text the appearance of being a bit more weathered and less new.

Our exploration of the **Materials** panel and the use of Substance 3D materials within Photoshop is nearly concluded. You have applied realistic materials to the composition background, the book cover, and the cover title text.

All that is needed now is to apply some tried-and-true traditional Photoshop techniques to your composition to increase the feeling of realism and tie everything together.

Adding Additional Elements and Styles

When looking at the overall composition in its current state, the materials look good...but something is missing. The items that compose the visual look of the composition—the book, the book title, and the background surface—do not look very integrated. To complete the realistic look you want, you are going to use a combination of gradient fills and layer styles and blend everything together in a more believable way.

Using the Drop Shadow Effect

You'll first turn your attention to the book cover and give a better sense that this is a real-life object by introducing a drop shadow effect.

1. Locate and select the original book cover layer, named *Cover*.

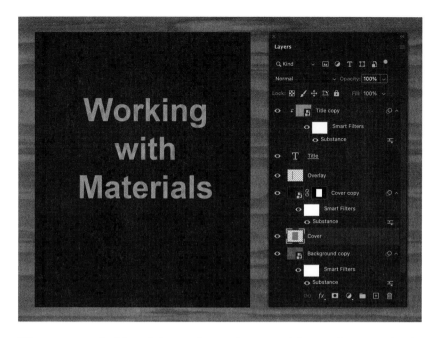

When you use the **Materials** panel to apply a material to any layer or selection, a duplicate of that layer is created. The original layer for each still exists within the **Layers** panel.

The cover and background look a bit flat right now—with no real indication of extra dimensionality. Let's change that.

2. Double-click the empty space in the *Cover* layer in the **Layers** panel—to the right of the layer name—to open the Layer Style dialog box.

3. Within the Layer Style dialog box, activate the Drop Shadow effect by clicking the checkbox to the left of its name in the left column. Be sure to click the name *Drop Shadow* as well—or you may not see the appropriate settings for this effect.

This activates a Drop Shadow effect with the default property values applied.

4. Make the following adjustments to the Drop Shadow properties to customize how it appears within your composition:

- Blend Mode: **Multiply**
- Drop Shadow Color: **#482f12**
- Opacity: **65**
- Angle: **120**
- Distance: **45**
- Spread: **0**
- Size: **60**

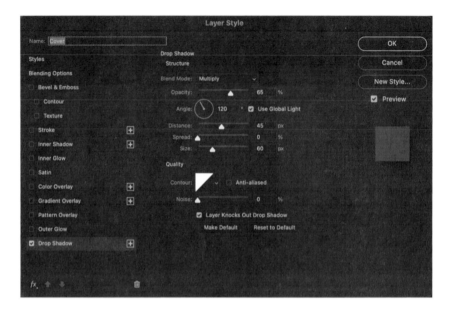

The changes you've made will be visible in the composition as long as the **Preview** checkbox is active.

5. Click **OK** to commit the changes and apply the Drop Shadow effect.

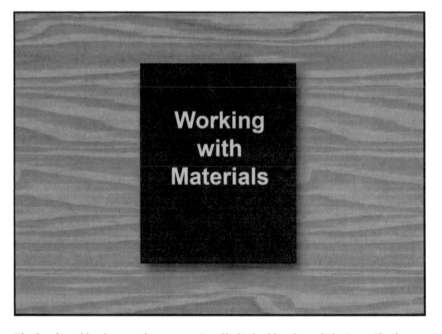

The book and background are now visually linked by the subtle Drop Shadow effect. This simple change really does pull everything together in a more realistic way.

You apply the Drop Shadow effect to the original *Cover* layer because the shadow extends from those pixels—visually outward—and can be seen as extending from the book cover in its entirety. Although you could just as easily add this effect to the copy of the layer with the material applied, this gives you more choices in how to blend the layers in the future.

For instance, with the drop shadow on its own layer, you have full control over this effect through the layer blend modes and opacity adjustments. If you were to apply the drop shadow to the same layer as the leather material, you would not be able to control these aspects independently.

Thinking things through and making these forward-looking determinations at the time of implementation can really help with additional decisions further along in the design process.

Using Gradient Blend

Let's also add a gradient blend to the book cover to simulate some directionality in lighting. The Lighting view within the **Materials** panel affects only the material's lighting in a uniform way, and by adding variance through a gradient, you can add realism to the object.

1. Create a new selection to confine the gradient you create by right-clicking (or Command/Ctrl-clicking) the existing mask within the *Cover copy* layer and choosing **Add Mask To Selection** from the menu that appears.

   A selection marquee appears, enclosing the book within the composition.

2. Create a new layer directly above the currently selected layer by clicking the **New Layer** icon at the bottom of the **Layers** panel, and name the new layer **Lighting**.

3. Ensure that **Foreground Color** is set to black (**#000000**) at the bottom of the toolbar.

4. Select the **Gradient tool** from the toolbar.

5. In the edit bar, choose the gradient preset named *Foreground to Transparent* from the Basics category. Ensure that **Radial Gradient** is selected and that the **Reverse** checkbox is selected.

This allows you to compose a radial gradient that is transparent in the center and gets darker toward the edges.

6. Create the gradient by clicking a bit within the upper-right portion of the book cover and dragging across at about a **140-degree** angle, with a resulting scale of about **55%** the canvas width. Release the mouse button to establish the gradient. You can adjust the scale property in the **Properties** panel after the gradient is established.

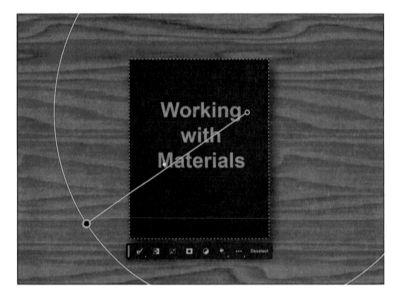

This creates the appearance of a hotspot across the book cover.

7. In the **Layers** panel, keep the blend mode set to **Normal** and take the **Opacity** value to **65%**.

The gradient is now complete, and the composition appears even more grounded in reality with this additional element.

Editing Existing Gradients

When creating a gradient in Photoshop, you can choose Gradient or Classic Gradient from the drop-down menu in the edit bar. When using a gradient (not a classic gradient), you can edit the parameters of your gradient, even after creating it, through the Properties panel.

Simply select the gradient layer and make any adjustments you need to achieve that perfect gradient!

Using Layer Styles

Finally, let's add some extra dimension to our golden title. It looks a bit flat right now, so let's introduce some bevel to the edges of the textured title characters via layer styles.

1. Select the *Title* layer to ensure the effects are added to the original layer and not to the *Title copy* layer that contains the Substance 3D material filter.

2. Double-click within the empty space in the *Title* layer in the **Layers** panel—to the right of the layer name—to open the Layer Style dialog box.

3. In the Layer Style dialog box, activate the Bevel & Emboss effect by clicking the checkbox to the left of its name in the left column. Ensure that the name *Bevel & Emboss* is selected as well to see the properties for this effect.

This activates a Bevel & Emboss effect with the default property values applied.

4. Make the following adjustments to the Bevel & Emboss properties to customize how the effect appears as applied to the title text:

   - Size: **5px**
   - Soften: **2px**

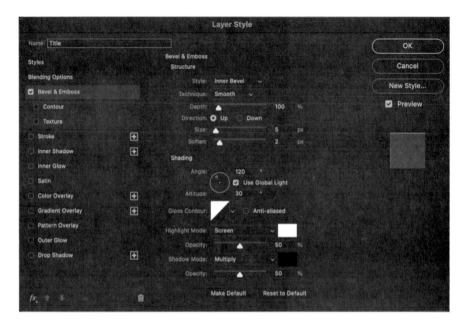

The text appears slightly beveled at the edges—assuming that the **Preview** checkbox is active. Leave the rest of the properties at their default values.

5. Click **OK** to commit your choices.

Your composition is now complete! You used both Substance 3D materials and traditional Photoshop workflows to texture and design a book.

This short project has been an excellent example of ways you can combine traditional Photoshop workflows with newer capabilities and Substance 3D materials.

CHAPTER 4

Producing 3D Models from Vector Shapes

Let's continue our exploration of 3D workflows within traditionally 2D-focused design software. In the previous chapter, we took an extensive look at working with 3D materials within a graphic composition using Adobe Photoshop. Adobe Illustrator includes access to 3D materials as well, with the addition of tools to create and export simple 3D models along with more robust lighting mechanics.

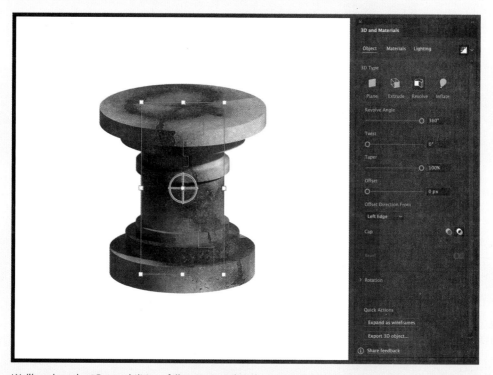

We'll explore the 3D capabilities of Illustrator in this chapter, with the goal of producing a 3D model that can be used in other software as well.

3D Tools in Adobe Illustrator

Although in this chapter you will be exploring the more modern Adobe Substance 3D–compatible workflows that are integrated with Illustrator, the software has had "classic" 3D capabilities for some time.

Classic 3D Tools

A lot of these tools still exist within Illustrator and can be accessed by choosing **Effect** > **3D and Materials** > **3D (Classic)** from the application menu. From this selection, you can choose **Extrude & Bevel (Classic)**, **Revolve (Classic)**, or **Rotate (Classic)** to open the respective options dialog box.

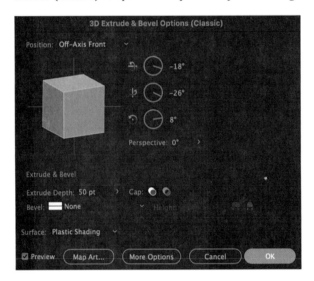

Each selection allows you to perform basic 3D transformations upon whatever vector content is currently selected. As you'll see in just a bit, these options correspond well with—and are vastly expanded upon through—modern, Substance 3D–driven workflows.

Modern 3D Tools

To access these new tools, you must select a vector object and then choose **Window** > **3D and Materials** from the application menu. This opens the **3D and Materials** panel, through which you can perform all the actions and workflows specified in this chapter.

This panel allows access to modern 3D tooling within Illustrator and includes three tab-based views:

- **Object:** This tab determines how three-dimensional transformations are applied to the selected vector object and allows you to tweak several parameters involving this transformation.

- **Materials:** This tab provides access to a set of materials that ship with Illustrator, and once a material has been applied, you can also adjust the various material properties. This is similar to what can be accessed within the Photoshop Materials panel.

- **Lighting:** Once a material has been chosen, you can adjust how the lighting is applied through this tab. Unlike the lighting capabilities in Photoshop, this feature allows the management of multiple lights.

You will be working with the **3D and Materials** panel throughout this chapter.

Accessing Additional Materials

While there is a good set of materials that come packaged within Illustrator, it is also possible to import your own materials or those that have been gathered from other sources—just as you saw with Photoshop.

- Click the **Add** button ➕ to browse for *.sbsar* files on your local computer.

- Click the Substance 3D **Assets** button 📦 to search for *.sbsar* files from the Substance 3D website.

- Click the Substance 3D **Community Assets** button 🔲 to search for *.sbsar* files from the Substance 3D Community Assets website.

Recall that we examined several ways to acquire and create materials and other assets in Chapter 2.

In the upper-right portion of the **3D and Materials** panel, you will find the **Render with Ray Tracing** toggle [icon]. Activating this toggle control reveals a dialog box that allows you to control how your content is rendered in 3D space.

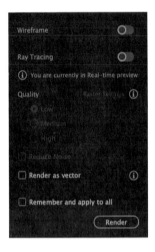

TIP It is better to switch Ray Tracing on only when you feel the need to view your design at higher quality with realistic lighting. If you keep Ray Tracing enabled throughout the design process, it can slow down your computer as you work.

Once Ray Tracing is activated, you can specify the quality of the render and whether to employ noise reduction to your content. Rendering your content with Ray Tracing enabled creates realistic lighting for your 3D objects. Keeping Ray Tracing disabled reduces the realism of your render but allows you to work faster in Illustrator.

We will examine the options presented in this overlay in greater depth toward the end of this chapter.

Working with the 3D and Materials Panel

To begin exploring 3D objects, materials, and lighting in Illustrator, you'll begin with a simple starter asset in the form of an Illustrator document file. The file exists to provide a common starting point to begin your work.

1. Open the file named *starter.ai* in Illustrator.

   The single artboard measures 576 px in both width and height and contains a single, empty layer.

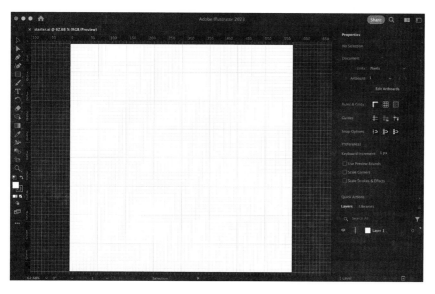

2. In the **Properties** panel, ensure that **Show Grid** 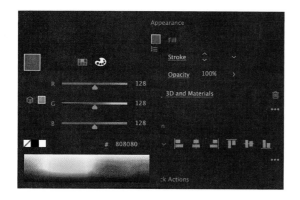 and **Snap to Grid** are toggled on.

   You will use the grid to more precisely draw your vector paths.

   With the file opened within Illustrator, you can begin exploring the **3D and Materials** panel. You'll first need to create a simple vector shape to work with.

3. Choose the **Rectangle** tool from the toolbar.

4. In the **Properties** panel, adjust the **Fill** and **Stroke** values so that the fill is a medium gray (**#808080**) and the stroke is set to **None**.

TIP Using a medium gray color like this will allow you to easily see both highlights and shadows once the shape is rendered to 3D.

This gives the rectangle that you create a simple appearance.

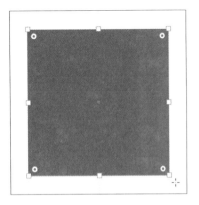

5. Draw a square against the grid, using the snapping options that you previously ensured were active to assist you.

   In my example, the square measures 144 px in both width and height.

   With a vector shape created, you can now use the **3D and Materials** panel to view differences between the various choices you have when it comes to 3D Type. This is located within the Object view of the **3D and Materials** panel and instructs Illustrator in what way you'd like to have your vector object translated into 3D.

   Let's explore these choices.

6. Select the newly created vector object and then choose **Window** > **3D and Materials** from the application menu.

   The **3D and Materials** panel appears with the Object view active as the default view. You are presented with four options for 3D Type: **Plane**, **Extrude**, **Revolve**, and **Inflate**. Clicking any of these four options translates the vector object and gives it a 3D appearance.

7. Select each of the four options to see what effect each has upon the square shape.

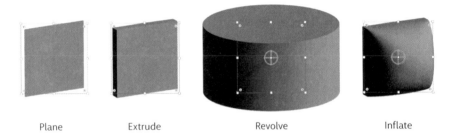

| Plane | Extrude | Revolve | Inflate |

As you can see through this exploration of different 3D Type choices, there is big difference in the result of each choice.

- **Plane:** Your 2D artwork remains a flat plane that can be manipulated in 3D space. This selection is unique, as the object retains its 2D appearance with only the perspective changing.

- **Extrude:** This option adds depth to your 2D object. You can specify the depth of the extrusion and specify additional properties, like a beveled edge, that create the perception of true 3D.

- **Revolve:** This option is great for creating simple 3D objects that appear as if formed on a physical lathe. It basically takes your shape and transforms it along a circular, sweeping path.

- **Inflate:** This option gives the effect of having your vector object puff out as though filled with air. The flat planes become inflated while the edges stay firm and clean.

These 3D Type choices can be applied to any object selection—including text.

Once a choice has been made, various properties become available that determine the appearance of your 3D object even further.

As you can see in the image, the options presented somewhat depend upon the chosen 3D type:

- **Depth:** Available for both Extrude and Inflate, the Depth value determines how much volume is added to the object. This can be set anywhere from 0 to 2000.

- **Revolve Angle:** Only available with Revolve, this parameter can have a value of anywhere from 0° to 360°. The default is 360°, which completes a filled, circular sweep on the object.

- **Twist:** This parameter adds a twisted appearance to the volume of the object. It can have a value of anywhere from 0° to 360°.

- **Taper:** This parameter adds to the volume of the object a tapered effect from 1% to 100%.

- **Offset:** Available for Revolve types only, this expands the revolution outward from the center, creating a void in the center in the process. The value can be set from 0pt to 1000pt.

- **Volume:** Available only with the Inflate 3D type, this determines the amount of visual inflation on the object and can be set from 1% to 100%.

- **Inflate Both Sides:** This is an additional option when working with the Inflate 3D type; it inflates both sides of the object rather than just one.

NOTE If you choose Plane for your 3D Type selection, you will not see any of these extra properties because it remains a 2D plane in 3D space.

- **Cap:** With the Cap button toggled on, you have a solid appearance to your object. With Cap set to off, the object appears hollow. This option is not available for the Plane 3D type.

Additionally, you can activate a **Bevel** option for Extrude 3D type objects that determines how the edges of the extrusion appear. All 3D types have access to a set of **Rotation** properties, which determine rotation along the x, y, and z axes.

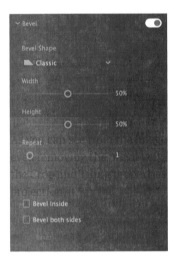 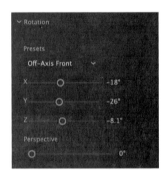

Bevel includes several presets that let you quickly apply a bevel type once this section has been activated. You can tweak the width and height, the repetition of the bevel, whether the inside is beveled, and whether to bevel both sides of the extrusion.

Rotation also contains a set of presets that let you dial in something quick and then provides access to the x, y, and z rotation values that can be adjusted manually.

NOTE Rotation properties are the only properties available to Plane 3D type objects.

You also get access to a gizmo overlay on the object itself, which you can use to adjust both Position and Rotation properties for the selected 3D object. Hovering over each visible axis of the gizmo reveals which property is affected by adjusting at that point.

Choosing any of these 3D types for your vector object creates a visual 3D rendering based upon the original path. That vector path still exists, even though its appearance has been altered.

This is an introduction to the 3D types available to you within the Object view. You will explore the Materials and Lighting views of the **3D and Materials** panel in the next section as you begin designing your custom 3D object.

Designing a More Complex 3D Object

Armed with a good grasp of the types of 3D objects you can create and their various properties, you'll now clear your starter document of any existing objects created during the initial exploration of the **3D and Materials** panel so that you can begin with a clean artboard. You can delete your existing objects, hide them through the **Properties** panel, or open a new version of *starter.ai* before you continue.

You will be designing an intricate columnar marble pillar in this project.

Designing a Cross-Section Path for 3D Revolve

As you saw previously, you can use any of the shape tools in Illustrator to draw a vector that you can convert to have a 3D appearance. In this project, you'll use the Pen tool, as it allows precise placement of anchor points along the drawing surface.

The idea is to create a cross-section that represents half of the object you intend to create. Try to visualize what it would look like in 3D while drawing the path. The following figure should help in visualizing how a 2D profile will translate into a 3D column.

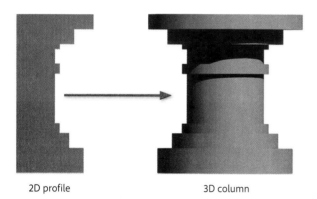

2D profile   3D column

Recall that you have several document-level settings activated to assist you in drawing your objects precisely across the grid. If you are unsure whether this is still the case, check the **Properties** panel to ensure that Show Grid ⊞ and Snap to Grid ▐▷ are toggled to the active state.

Let's draw a more complex shape that represents one half of a column.

1. Choose the **Pen** tool 🖊 from the toolbar and ensure that the **Fill** and **Stroke** settings from before are still active.

   The fill should be a medium gray (**#808080**) with the stroke set to **None**.

2. Recall that the artboard is a perfect square. Try to envision what you'd like the column to look like, and begin by placing an anchor point in a spot close to the top of the artboard that gives you a lot of room to begin drawing.

Moving the **Pen** tool across the grid with your initial anchor point in place will provide a preview of your path.

3. Use the grid to easily click to place additional anchor points that represent the top of the column, and continue placing additional points to build out the intricate sides of the column as well.

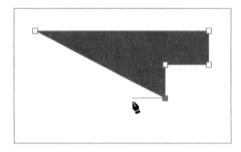

Simply clicking at various points is enough for this exercise, but if you want to use anchor point handles and Bezier curves, feel free to do so.

4. Continue placing anchor points along the length of the column in whatever formation you desire until you get to what will be the column's base.

The **Snap to Grid** option  you previously activated should make precisely aligning each point very simple.

5. Complete the column cross-section by traveling back upward to click the original anchor point, closing the path.

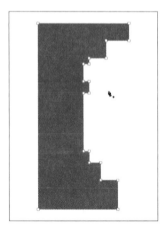

NOTE If your drawing deviates from what is represented in the image, that is totally fine. You can design your column however you like.

You should be left with what will serve as the cross-section of a complex column. The object will be a single closed path.

Creating a 3D Object and Applying Materials

Now that you have a vector object to work with, you'll apply a 3D Type transformation onto it to give it the appearance of a fully three-dimensional column. This is like what you did with the square shape in the previous exploration of the **3D and Materials** panel.

You'll now convert your vector shape into a 3D object.

1. Ensure that your new path is selected in the **Layers** panel by either selecting it on the Canvas with the **Selection** tool or clicking the circle next to it in the **Layers** panel.

   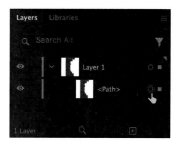

   A colored square appears on any selected objects in the **Layers** panel.

2. Open the **3D and Materials** panel by choosing **Window** > **3D and Materials** from the application menu.

   You can also open the panel through the **Choose an Effect** option *fx.* in the **Properties** panel.

3. Choose **Revolve** from the 3D Type options in the Object view of the panel.

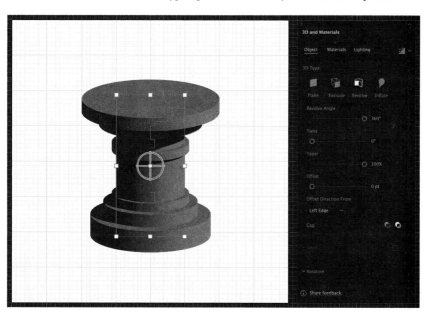

The object takes on a 3D appearance by rendering a full 360° column from your simple vector cross-section and applying a Rotation preset. You might have to scroll down in the **3D and Materials** panel to see the Rotation presets. The default Rotation preset is **Off-Axis Front**, which is a perfect view for our intentions. In fact, you are not going to adjust any attributes within the Object view of the **3D and Materials** panel.

Notice that the vector path outline is still visible when the object is selected, indicating the original form. In the **Properties** panel, the selected object retains the definition of a Path object with all the expected attributes. The 3D appearance is presented as an effect that is applied to this object.

Now that the Revolve effect has been added, you can move to the next step and apply a 3D material to give your column an even more realistic appearance. Now that your vector drawing is complete, you are finished with the document grid.

4. Hide the grid by selecting **View** > **Hide Grid** from the application menu, or you can deselect the column to expose document properties within the **Properties** panel and hide the grid by clicking the **Hide Grid** icon ▦ .

   This gives you a less cluttered view as you work.

5. Ensure that the column is once again selected, and in the **3D and Materials** panel, switch to the Materials view from the set of tabs at the top of the panel.

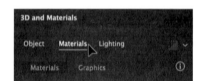

   The Materials view displays several built-in Substance 3D materials for you to choose from.

6. Locate the material named *Calcutta Marble* and click it to apply the material to your object.

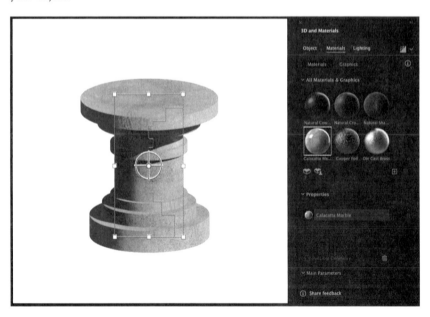

The column takes on the appearance of a veined marble stone.

Now that a material has been applied, you can explore the Properties section of the Materials view. The Properties section is beneath the Materials section, so you may need to scroll down in the **3D and Materials** panel to view it. All Substance 3D materials have their own unique set of parameters that you can adjust to customize the material.

7. Make the following adjustments to give the marble a more distinct look:

- Resolution: **2048px**
- Veins Color: **#681D00**
- Veins Color Intensity: **0.8**
- Stain Color: **#2C3F01**

These adjustments give the marble a much more distinct appearance. It renders at a higher resolution, has more visual contrast between the base marble and the veining, and looks weathered and moss-stained from exposure to the elements.

Even though the Materials view is nearly identical to what you see in Photoshop, there is one major difference. You may have noticed that there are two sub-views within the Materials view: Materials—which is the default—and Graphics.

Graphics use symbols in your document to apply visuals to the 3D object in a way that conforms to the 3D dimensions of the selected object. Any artwork that you would like to use in this way must be converted to a symbol first. Note that a graphic is placed visually above any chosen material. In this way, they act like decals or stickers.

You can also simply drag artwork from your canvas into the Graphics section of the **3D and Materials** panel, and they will be converted to symbols automatically and be ready for immediate use.

If you have used Adobe Dimension or Substance 3D Stager before, you will be familiar with the placement, rotation, and scale controls that are present in Illustrator as well.

Adjusting Object Lighting

The default lighting preset looks good with our column and material choices, but you will often find when working with 3D in Illustrator that changes in lighting can provide the exact look that you want. Let's, therefore, explore the Lighting view of the **3D and Materials** panel.

Just as when you switched the view from Object to Materials, all you need to do is click the Lighting tab at the top of the panel to access the corresponding view.

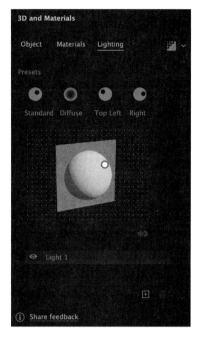
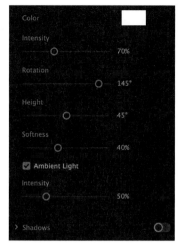

The Lighting view displays the default lighting preset along with all properties dialed in to conform to that preset. You can use presets as a starting point for any lighting adjustments you'd like to make. The default preset is named *Standard*.

Aside from the Standard preset, you also have access to Diffuse, Top Left, and Right. Don't be worried about messing up any settings in your exploration, because you can always revert to any of these presets and all corresponding attribute values will be set to conform to that preset.

As you choose different presets, keep an eye on the properties that appear in the lower portion of the panel and also how these presets affect your column object on the canvas.

Let's go over each of these properties and how their values affect the appearance of the selected 3D object:

- **Color:** The color of the light itself. The default color is white.

- **Intensity:** This determines the brightness of the selected light, which can be set from 0% to 100%.

- **Rotation:** This rotates the light around the selected object, determining where the light is being projected from.

- **Height:** This determines how close the light is to the object.

- **Softness:** This determines how diffusely the light spreads across the selected object, from 0% to 100%.

- **Ambient Light:** This checkbox determines whether to apply a global ambient light.

- **Intensity (Ambient Light):** If Ambient Light is being used, this controls the intensity from 0% to 200%.

- **Shadows:** This toggle switch determines whether the light will cast shadows from the selected object.

- **Position (Shadows):** When Shadows is active, this determines whether the shadows are cast behind or below the selected object.

- **Distance from Object (Shadows):** When Shadows is active, this property adjusts the distance the shadow appears from the selected object.

- **Shadow Bounds (Shadows):** When Shadows is active, a value of from 10% to 400% will determine the shadows' boundary. Setting Softness to a higher value can create a rather hard edge to a cast shadow, and increasing the Shadow Bounds value can sometimes help alleviate this somewhat.

In addition to these options, you can create additional lights, each with their own lighting properties. As you create additional lights, you can control the parameters of each light individually, allowing for some very complex lighting scenarios.

While text descriptions are fine, getting hands-on with these properties better reinforces exactly how they affect the lighting applied to your object. Explore a bit before moving on, and remember that you can always reset everything by selecting one of the presets at the top of the panel.

Rendering Options

Once you are finished with your 3D objects—choosing a 3D Type, applying materials, and adjusting your lighting—you'll want to look at the various render settings that are available. These settings were briefly mentioned at the beginning of the chapter.

In the upper right of the **3D and Materials** panel is an icon with a small arrow next to it. Clicking the arrow reveals the Render Settings overlay, through which you can access the various properties of your full render.

TIP To view lighting most effectively—and especially the rendering of shadows—you will want to activate Ray Tracing for your object, which is covered in the next section.

NOTE These lights are bound to the selected 3D object rather than to all 3D objects within your document. If you want the lighting to match across multiple objects, you'll need to ensure you use the same settings for each one.

TIP Be sure to click the arrow and not the icon, as the icon will toggle a full render of your object.

As is visible within the Render Settings overlay, you can choose some primary options to render your objects. Each results in a different appearance for the full render.

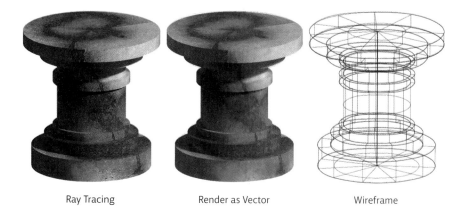

| Ray Tracing | Render as Vector | Wireframe |

Let's briefly examine these three render choices:

- **Ray Tracing:** This is the best choice for photorealistic renders that can fully support lighting and shadow.

- **Render as Vector:** This option renders the object as resolution-independent vector content. It excludes raster and gradient content.

- **Wireframe:** This renders the object as a wireframe only.

We will now render our column with high-quality Ray Tracing:

1. Create a high-quality, photorealistic render of your column by setting the following:

   - Ensure the **Ray Tracing** option is toggled to the on state.

   - **Quality** should be set to **High**.

   - **Reduce Noise** should be enabled.

2. Close the Render Settings overlay by clicking outside it.

3. Activate the **Render with Ray Tracing** toggle icon to actually render the object.

   A dialog box appears with a progress bar that informs you of the rendering progress.

TIP You can also adjust the raster settings through the option included here to affect the resolution, color, and background for the ray-traced raster image render.

TIP You can also initiate a render through the Render button within the overlay.

With the Render with Ray Tracing option active, any changes you make to the object will trigger another render process. It is a good idea to temporarily disable this when making changes in order to work faster and then render again once complete.

At this point, you can integrate your rendered object into another artboard, continue designing around it, or use any other traditional Illustrator workflows to complete a design. Just as with any Illustrator document, you can save as a PDF, export to bitmap images, or export to any other file formats that you may be used to working with in the software.

Exporting 3D Models

You are dealing with the creation of 3D objects in Illustrator, so why not export these objects as real 3D file formats for use outside Illustrator as well? The **3D and Materials** panel makes this easy to do.

1. Within the Object view of the **3D and Materials** panel, scroll to the very bottom to find two quick actions for your object. Click **Export 3D object**.

   Choosing the **Expand as Wireframes** quick action would flatten your object into a wireframe that is no longer editable in the **3D and Materials** panel.

   Choosing **Export 3D object** summons the **Asset Export** panel, adds the object to export, and provides a single USDA file format entry within the export settings.

2. Choose either **OBJ** or **GLTF** as your file format for export. While **USDA** is the default, **OBJ** and **GLTF** are more common, and we can use these formats in additional Adobe software more readily.

   You can even add them all as additional export formats so that you will have access to a variety of 3D file formats depending upon what software you want to work with outside Illustrator.

   There are three file types you can render using this export method that are associated with 3D applications:

   - **USDA/USDZ:** Developed by Pixar and Apple, this is used primarily in augmented reality applications. It is now open source and becoming increasingly common but has very little support across Adobe Creative Cloud software. USDZ is a zipped version of USDA.

- **OBJ:** A nearly universal format for 3D geometry, this can be used directly within Substance 3D Stager, Adobe Aero, Adobe After Effects, and Adobe Animate.

- **GLTF:** This open-source format is often used on the web. This format can be used in Substance 3D Stager, Adobe After Effects, and Adobe Animate.

3. Once you've chosen the formats to export to, click the **Export** button to begin the file export process.

   A Browse dialog box appears that allows you to define a location in your file system for the exported files.

4. Navigate to the location you want to export your file(s) to.

   Once you choose the location, the export process begins.

   A Progress dialog box appears and exports the 3D object from your document into the distinct file formats you've chosen.

NOTE Recall that we examined these 3D file types and others in Chapter 1.

Of course, you can always export as non-3D file formats as well—through this same workflow. Just choose non-3D file formats from the **Asset Export** panel.

When you look at the location chosen for your file exports, you will find that the exported file formats are available to use outside Illustrator.

Depending upon the file format, you may find that you have a single file or a set of files that compose the chosen export. These often consist of the primary *.usda* or *.obj* file alongside various materials, textures, and so on.

With that, you have gone through the entire process of designing vector content, transforming paths into 3D objects, applying materials to them, adjusting those material properties and associated lighting, making render setting choices, and exporting objects for use in other software.

CHAPTER 5

Compositing Motion Graphics in 3D

In this chapter, we move beyond static experiences to design across time using assets created in Adobe Illustrator and realized through Adobe After Effects. We'll import content into a new composition and translate 2D artwork across 3D space. Following this, we will create motion with a 3D-enabled camera, traditional keyframing techniques, and 3D lighting.

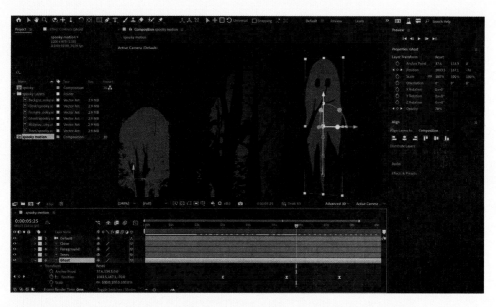

We'll explore several methods for rendering motion design through both Adobe Media Encoder and Adobe After Effects via a native render workflow.

Working with 2D Content in 3D Space

In Chapter 1, we looked at two ways of working in 3D space. The first was through the manipulation of flat graphics in perspective to give the appearance of 3D, and the second was to use actual 3D models. After Effects is capable of both.

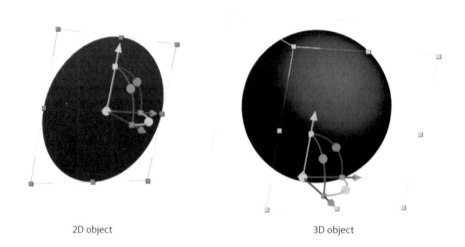

2D object   3D object

This is expressed well in this image. Both the 2D object and 3D object exist within an After Effects composition. Their appearance and the related controls inform you of their nature. The 2D object, when selected, exhibits a flat transformation rectangle around it, while the 3D object appears as though contained within a three-dimensional transformation cube. This difference is the projected volume of the object in 3D space.

This chapter explores the use of 2D object types in 3D space, starting with the use of 2D illustrations on a 3D canvas within an After Effects composition.

Setting Up a Project in After Effects

Although After Effects includes some drawing tools, most designers rely on an external application—such as Illustrator—to create their artwork. In this exercise, you will import a multilayered Illustrator document into After Effects to create a motion design using 3D layers and the camera within a composition.

I've prepared an Illustrator document for you to use for these exercises.

1. Locate the file *spooky.ai* in the book's exercise files and open it in Illustrator to understand its composition.

   The document includes a single artboard with different designs spread across six distinct layers. They work together to establish the design of a spooky, forested scene bathed in violet and black. The forest floor is hilly, and trees sprout up along the wooded expanse. A little ghost appears at the right of the frame.

When you're using Illustrator files in After Effects, layer organization and order are incredibly important.

2. Look at the **Layers** panel and take stock of the document content structure. If you do not see the **Layers** panel, choose **Window** > **Layers** from the application menu.

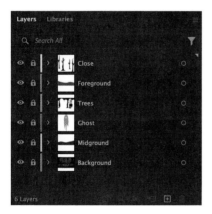

Six distinct layers are named in accordance with either the specific content within or their intended placement relative to the viewer. All these layers are locked, but you can twirl them open to view the contents if desired.

3. Now that you are familiar with the document structure, exit Illustrator and launch After Effects.

Importing Illustrated Artwork

Once you launch After Effects, you will see the home screen, which prompts you to either open an existing project or create a new one.

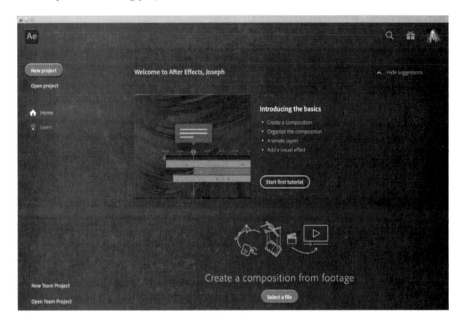

Let's set up a new project and import our artwork.

TIP To reset any work-
space to its original
configuration, click the
workspace options icon
■ to the right of the
workspace name and
choose Reset To Saved
Layout from the menu
that appears.

1. From the home screen, click **New Project**.

    The home screen disappears, and you enter After Effects proper. You are presented with the last workspace chosen; the **Default** workspace is what we will be using in this book.

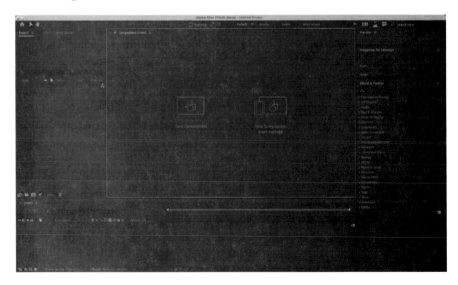

2. Choose **File** > **Import** > **File** from the application menu.

   A system file browser appears.

3. Browse to the location of *spooky.ai* and select it.

4. Adjust the import options by choosing **Composition – Retain Layer Sizes** from the **Import As** menu.

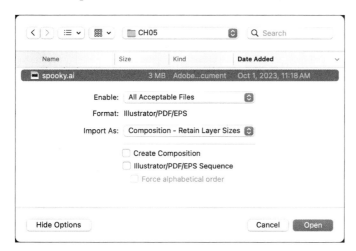

By choosing the **Composition – Retain Layer Sizes** option, you are instructing After Effects to import each layer at its actual content size and not at the size of the original artboard. This makes each layer much easier to manipulate in 3D space. These layers will be included in the same order in which they appear in the original file.

5. Click **Open** to import the Illustrator file into a new After Effects composition based on the original artboard dimensions.

   You have successfully imported the artwork into your project in such a way that it will be most accessible when working in a 3D-enabled canvas.

6. Look at the **Project** panel.

   All the content you imported from Illustrator now exists here, in your project. Initially, you see a composition named **spooky** (named after the imported document) along with a folder named **spooky Layers**.

7. Expand the **spooky Layers** folder.

   You can see that each distinct layer from the original document has been imported as a separate asset.

NOTE It is not necessary to click the Create Composition checkbox when importing content in this manner, because a composition will always be created for you.

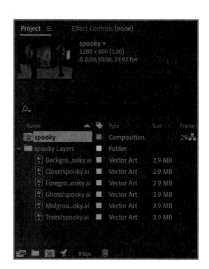

8. Double-click the **spooky** composition to open it in the project.

The artwork appears in the **Composition** panel, and all six layers are nested in the composition and shown in the **Timeline** panel at the bottom of the window.

Everything is now prepared and ready to be worked on.

Adjusting Composition Settings

It's always a good idea to ensure that your composition settings are exactly as you want them before performing any motion design across the composition timeline. Depending on several factors, including the imported source material used to create the composition and your previous work in After Effects, you may need to adjust some of these settings to match your intentions as a designer.

1. Choose **Composition** > **Composition Settings** from the application menu.

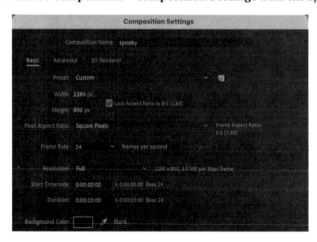

The **Composition Settings** dialog box appears.

2. Verify that the following property values are set:

- Width: **1280px**

- Height: **800px**

- Pixel Aspect Ratio: **Square Pixels**

- Frame Rate: **24fps**

- Start Timecode: **0:00:00:00**

- Duration: **0:00:10:00**

- Background Color: **Black**

TIP If your composition was previously set to a different duration, you will need to adjust your layer content. Select all layers, go to Layer > Time > Time Stretch, and set the New Duration value to 0:00:10:00 to match the composition settings.

These values ensure that your composition settings match those that you will see in the following steps. They create a composition that measures 1280x800 pixels, with a timeline that is 10 seconds in length, and with each second composed of 24 individual frames. The composition resolution matches the Illustrator artboard resolution exactly.

Saving Your Project

You'll now save your project file before beginning work in the composition. Saving the project ensures that if anything happens while you work you do not have to redo all the work you've already done. It also allows you to step away from the project and resume your work later.

1. From the application menu, choose **File** > **Save As** > **Save As**.

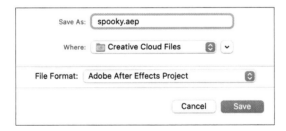

A system-level save dialog box appears.

2. Enter a name for your project, choose a location on your local file system, and be sure that **Adobe After Effects Project** is chosen from the **File Format** menu.

3. Click **Save** to save your project file and return to the composition.

Your project is now saved and ready to work on. You should save often by choosing File > Save or using the keyboard shortcut Command+S (macOS) or Control+S (Windows).

Designing in 3D Space

Although much of the content produced with After Effects is either visual effects for video or 2D motion graphics, the ability to work with 3D is becoming increasingly popular. Only a few years ago, the entire set of 3D tools and workflows was updated and modernized.

Working with 3D Layers

As you will see in Chapter 9, it is entirely possible to work with true 3D models in an After Effects composition, but for now, you'll manipulate a combination of 2D Illustrator content in 3D space in After Effects. To achieve this, you must declare your imported 2D layers as 3D using the 3D layer toggle.

Let's explore how to enable 3D layers and their associated controls.

1. In the timeline, click the **Enable 3D Layer** toggle  for each layer that was brought in from Illustrator.

   This enables the 3D composition properties for each layer and allows you to manipulate additional 3D transform properties.

2. Click the *Ghost* layer to select it and make sure the **Selection** tool ▶ (located in the upper-left corner of the application window) is selected.

   A 3D gizmo appears as an overlay atop the little ghost in the composition window.

   If you find it difficult to select the ghost from the **Composition** window, you can also select the *Ghost* layer in the timeline to achieve the same result.

   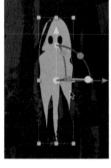

   NOTE If you need a refresher on 3D gizmo controls, refer to Chapter 1, which describes 3D gizmo controls and how to use them to manipulate content in 3D space.

3. Using the gizmo, manipulate the position, scale, and rotation of the ghost to get a feel for these controls.

   Adjusting these properties through the gizmo can drastically alter the orientation of the little ghost in 3D space.

   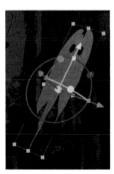

Using the 3D Gizmo Overlay

As a refresher, let's examine what the various colors and shapes represent when using the gizmo overlay.

The three colors represent the three axes available to use in 3D space:

- **x axis** = red
- **y axis** = green
- **z axis** = blue

The shapes that appear along each colored control represent the three orientation properties that you can adjust using the gizmo:

- **Cone** = position
- **Cube** = scale
- **Sphere** = rotation

In the lower left of the Composition window, each axis is labeled with a specific color as well.

4. Open the *Ghost* layer properties from within the timeline.

   In addition to **Transform** properties, a 3D layer also includes properties for **Geometry Options** and **Material Options**.

5. Open the **Transform** properties.

   In this category, the 3D layers include an additional set of properties—including **Orientation**—which is what you have been manipulating with the gizmo.

   Before moving on, you'll reset the orientation changes you made while exploring the gizmo.

6. Right-click the **Orientation** property and choose **Reset** from the menu to reset all Orientation properties to **0°**.

The 3D orientation properties of the *Ghost* layer are now reset to their original values. You'll adjust some of these again later, but for now you want everything set to 0° for the next steps in this project.

Spacing Layers for Parallax Movement

Now that you understand how to enable layers for 3D manipulation and to manipulate the orientation properties in each 3D-enabled layer, you will space them in a staggered way across the z-axis. This will have the effect of placing certain layers closer to the viewer and others farther away, which can create an interesting parallax movement when adding motion across the timeline.

Additionally, manipulating the z-axis of your layers in 3D space can have the effect of overriding the layer stacking order displayed in the timeline.

1. You are currently using the **Default** camera view. Switch the camera view by choosing **View** > **Switch 3D View** > **Top**, or click the **3D View Popup** control in the lower right of the composition window to access the same options.

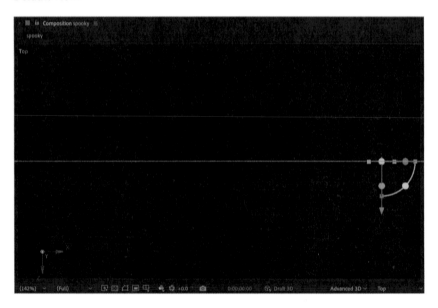

The 3D view shifts to display the 3D composition from the top, looking down on all layers from above instead of face-on as it was represented in the Default view.

> **NOTE** In the image, the *Ghost* layer is still selected, so the 3D gizmo remains visible. If nothing were selected, you would see only the line.

All 3D layers have the same z-axis position of 0 and so appear as a simple, thin line across the center of the composition window. You will adjust these positions to provide distance between each layer across the z-axis of the 3D canvas.

2. Select the layer named *Close* in the layers area of the timeline and position the **Selection** tool over the blue cone of the gizmo that appears.

3. Drag the cone downward to displace the z position by 160 to a value of **–160**, bringing the layer much closer to the viewer. The values of all three dimensions appear as a small overlay label as you drag.

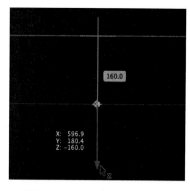

It may seem odd that the value is displayed in negative numbers, but this is simply because you have shifted it 160 units across the z-axis in that direction. If you were to shift it in the other direction from the starting value of 0, it would be a positive number but visually shifted farther away from the viewer.

4. Release the mouse button to commit the change.

5. Select the *Foreground* layer from the layers section of the timeline and drag it until the label for the z-axis displays a value of **–120**.

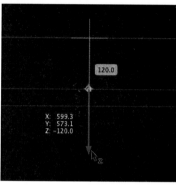

Note again that there are two values displayed: the amount you shifted the object and the new orientation along the z-axis.

6. Continue displacing the remaining 3D layers by adjusting their z-axis values:

- Trees: **–90**

- Ghost: **–70**

- Midground: **–50**

- Background: **–2**

They will now exhibit different z-axis positions spaced out from one another and will be visibly separate from one another when viewed in the **Composition** window.

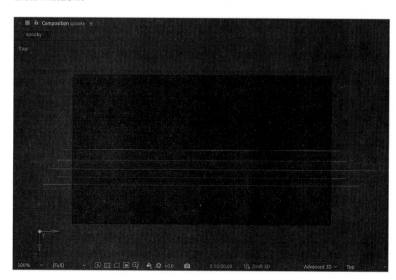

Notice that the layers display different widths because you imported them while retaining their specific dimensions by choosing **Composition – Retain Layer Sizes**. This is particularly apparent in the *Ghost* layer.

7. Switch back to the **Default** camera view by choosing **View** > **Switch 3D View** > **Default** from the application menu or by clicking the **3D View Popup** control in the lower right of the **Composition** window.

   The camera view reverts to the default, and you can see all the artwork clearly once again.

8. Choose the **Orbit** tool 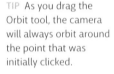 and drag around the Composition window to view the 3D parallax effect you created by changing the z position of each layer.

TIP As you drag the Orbit tool, the camera will always orbit around the point that was initially clicked.

   Notice that the outlines of each layer appear outside the composition frame, indicating how much content you have available to you when adjusting the camera.

You will now reset the camera view.

9. Choose **View** > **Reset Default Camera** from the application menu to return the camera view to how it appeared before you used the Orbit tool.

Next, you'll adjust the camera across the timeline to create parallax motion.

Using Draft 3D View

With Draft 3D view activated, After Effects uses a real-time renderer for any changes and updates to your 3D composition. This view is much faster than the normal 3D render view and enables you to work more quickly and without as much lag, but the render quality will not be as good.

- To enable Draft 3D view, locate the **Draft 3D** toggle ⬚ Draft 3D below the **Composition** panel and click it.

  The view of your composition will change to allow fast previews in 3D space, and you will get the additional benefits of being able to view content that extends past the composition frame and being able to view the ground plane grid.

- To view the ground plane, click the **Ground Plane** toggle ⊞ with Draft 3D view activated. You may need to adjust the camera view to see the ground plane.

- To view content that extends past the composition frame, click the **Extended Viewer** toggle ▣ with Draft 3D activated. By long-pressing the **Extended Viewer** toggle, you get access to a slider that lets you adjust the opacity of the extended content.

Both toggles are located immediately to the right of the Draft 3D toggle.

Animating Your 3D Composition Elements

Now that you understand the 3D canvas and how to work across all three dimensions in a composition, it's time to set the imported assets in motion.

You are going to animate only two objects in this project—the camera and the ghost—but the animation generated across the 3D composition will make it appear as if everything is in motion due to how you have set up the layers across the z-axis.

Animating the 3D Camera

You will give motion to the camera, which will have the effect of making the 3D layers apparently move and shift. The camera is the only object you move to create this 3D effect.

Creating Project "Bookmarks"

Your content has been imported and configured within the composition. Since you'll now be exploring motion, you may want to duplicate your composition so that you have a nice place to start from in case anything gets goofed up while you work.

1. In your **Project** panel, select the **Spooky** composition and choose **Edit > Duplicate** from the application menu. You can also use the keyboard shortcut Command+D (macOS) or Control+D (Windows).

2. Select the new composition and press **Return** (macOS) or **Enter** (Windows) to rename the composition to match what you are working on.

    I suggest simply renaming it **Spooky Motion** for clarity.

It isn't necessary to make a copy like this as you work, but it is especially helpful because multiple compositions in various stages of completion can act as convenient bookmarks to return to should anything bad happen.

If you didn't reset the camera view after exploring Draft 3D or any other feature, choose View > Reset Default 2 Camera from the application menu.

To animate the camera view, you must first create a new camera object in order to set keyframes on its properties across the timeline.

1. Choose **View > Create Camera from 3D View** from the application menu to create a new camera from the current view.

    A camera layer is created from the current 3D view and is named

after that view. Since you created the camera from the Default view, the name *Default 2* is assigned to the layer.

2. Ensure that the Default 2 camera view is active by selecting it from the menu in the lower right of the **Composition** panel.

If the correct camera view is not selected in this way, you will not see the adjustments you make to that camera's properties.

3. Drag the blue playhead across the timeline to **02s** (the 2-second mark).

TIP If you cannot clearly see the 02s mark in the timeline, you can adjust the zoom level by using the zoom slider at the bottom of the timeline or by adjusting the time readout in the upper left of the layers section by dragging it until it displays 0:00:02:00.

This is where you want your camera movement to begin.

4. Twirl open the camera layer properties by clicking the small properties toggle to the left of the *Default 2* camera layer.

5. Twirl open the nested **Transform** category.

Next, you will adjust a set of camera properties across the timeline.

6. Activate the **Stopwatch** toggle to the left of both the **Point of Interest** and **Position** properties.

Two diamond-shaped keyframes holding information for the camera are added at the 2-second mark.

7. Drag the playhead across the timeline to **08s** (the 8-second mark).

This is where you want the camera movement to complete. You will have the camera zoom in, shift across the woods, and pivot to focus on the little ghost. This will be a dramatic movement that takes advantage of the layers residing across different z-axis values.

8. Use a combination of the **Orbit**, **Move**, and **Pan** tools  to adjust the camera view to match the image.

02s   08s

Not only are you moving the camera directly ahead and to the right, but you are also shifting it across to the side and adjusting the point of interest.

9. Enter the following property values directly, for precision:

   • Point of Interest: **868, 160, 110**

   • Position: **1370, 80, −620**

   The rough camera movement is now complete.

10. To view the motion, move the playhead to the beginning of the timeline and press the spacebar.

   The camera moves and pivots with obvious parallax movement across the layers.

The parallax effect is exactly what you were trying to achieve, but the movement is very linear and stiff right now. In the next section, you will create much more engaging and dynamic motion by staggering keyframes and adding custom eases with the Graph Editor.

Adjusting the Timing

To adjust the motion to be more dynamic and interesting, you can use several workflow tweaks that are common to After Effects.

To make the movement even more interesting, you'll perform additional adjustments.

1. Drag the Point of Interest keyframe from 08s to **05s**.

This has the effect of staggering the motion across the properties, having the point-of-interest shift occur halfway through the camera position movement and adding dynamism to the camera motion.

NOTE When moving a keyframe to a different point along the timeline, the properties assigned to that keyframe remain the same. Only the timing between keyframes is affected.

The second adjustment you will make is to the easing properties between keyframes so that the motion is given more weight and emphasis at certain points instead of being boring and linear.

2. Select the keyframes associated with the **Position** property by dragging a selection rectangle across them both or by clicking the word **Position** under the **Transform** property group.

Both keyframes aligned with the **Position** property are selected and appear with a blue outline.

3. Choose **Animation** > **Keyframe Assistant** > **Easy Ease** from the application menu or press the **F9** key on your keyboard.

This applies an Easy ease to both keyframes, creating motion that starts off slow, becomes quicker toward the middle, and ends slowly. Easing can bring a real physicality and weight to your motion design.

We can tell that easing has been applied because the keyframes are now shaped like small hourglasses rather than diamonds.

To preview your changes, move the playhead to the beginning of the timeline and play it. See how much smoother and more organic the motion appears with easing applied to the camera movement.

You can add a bit of easing to the **Point of Interest** property as well. Let's do this directly in the Graph Editor before returning to the timeline view.

Easing and the Graph Editor

If you'd like a more detailed view of how easing works, you'll need to open the Graph Editor.

Locate the **Graph Editor** toggle 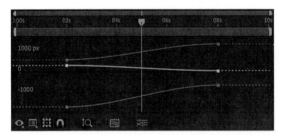 above the layers in the timeline, and then click the toggle to activate the Graph Editor.

The timeline changes to display the Graph Editor view where your keyframes previously appeared.

The Graph Editor displays the selected property, including all dimensions if the property is multidimensional, as the Position property is. The multidimensional Position property is separated into X position, Y position, and Z position, as indicated by the colored lines.

Click the **Choose Graph Type and Options** button 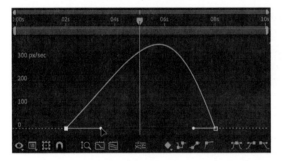 below the graph and select **Edit Speed Graph** from the menu that appears. This transforms the view from the three position properties to a single-speed graph that appears as an arc.

Note that the arc path includes anchor points at each end. These are your keyframes, and in the Graph Editor they can be manipulated just like anchor points in Illustrator. Handles protrude from each anchor point, which allows you to adjust the Bezier curves that influence the strength of your path and the motion that it informs in order to speed up or slow down the motion. Dragging a handle closer to or farther from the center of the arced path creates a more or less severe ease, respectively, at the beginning or end of the motion.

To return to the default view, click the **Choose Graph Type and Options** button again and choose **Edit Value Graph** from the menu.

4. Select the **Point of Interest** property label to display all three dimensions in the Graph Editor.

5. Select the **Point of Interest** property label a second time to select all keyframes associated with that property.

6. Click the **Easy Ease** button  below the Graph Editor to quickly apply an Easy ease to all three property dimensions at once.

NOTE The Point of Interest is set to the center of the composition by default. Most camera types will focus on the Point of Interest unless additional adjustments are made, such as those in this project.

---

7. Click the **Graph Editor** button ⬚ once more to exit the Graph Editor.

You return to the regular timeline view and the previously diamond-shaped keyframes now appear as little hourglasses, indicating that easing has been applied to them.

Even a small bit of keyframe staggering and easing to create variance within your motion can go a long way toward making the camera movement more interesting for the viewer.

Animating the Ghost

With the camera movement and subsequent parallax animation in place, you will now give life to the little ghost. The ghost will appear a few seconds into the composition and hover up and down between the trees as his form fades in and out. This will all occur in parallel with the camera movement, creating a scene filled with dynamic, engaging movement in 3D space.

Let's bring this little friend to life.

1. Move the playhead across the composition timeline to the **03s** mark.

   The time in the upper left of the timeline panel should read 0:00:03:00.

TIP The default format for time display in After Effects is 0:00:00:00, which indicates hours, minutes, seconds, and frames.

---

2. Select the *Ghost* layer in the timeline.

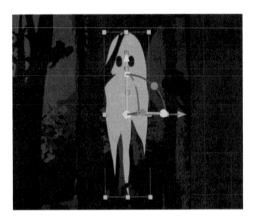

A transform rectangle and 3D gizmo controls appear on the ghost to indicate it is selected.

3. Click the Properties toggle ▶ to the left of the *Ghost* layer to open the property groups for the layer.

4. Open the **Transform** group to expose the individual **Transform** properties.

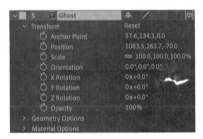

You now have access to the **Position** and **Opacity** properties and can establish keyframes across the timeline for both properties.

5. Click the **Stopwatch** toggle to the left of both the **Position** and **Opacity** properties to create keyframes for these properties.

The initial keyframes have been set for both properties at the 03s mark and appear as small diamonds in the timeline.

To make the ghost hover up and down, you will adjust the **Position** property along the y-axis.

6. Move the playhead to a new time and adjust the value as needed to create additional keyframes.

The following times and keyframe values for the y position (displayed as the middle value of the **Position** property) are provided as a guide; you do not have to be exact in placement or value. Recall that the first keyframe already exists.

- 03s 00f: **263**
- 05s 15f: **161**
- 07s 15f: **226**
- 10s 00f: **188**

You may also want to use the green cone on the gizmo overlay to adjust these properties. Either method results in the same thing—a change in the y position of the ghost.

To make the ghost fade in and out of view, you will make adjustments to the **Opacity** property.

7. Create additional keyframes at every second mark and alternate between a value of **0%** and **80%** to fade the little ghost in and out as he hovers.

The following times and keyframe values for the **Opacity** percentage are provided as a guide; you do not need to be exact. Again, recall that the first keyframe already exists.

- 03s 00f: **0%**
- 04s 00f: **80%**
- 05s 00f: **0%**
- 06s 00f: **80%**
- 07s 00f: **0%**
- 08s 00f: **80%**
- 09s 00f: **0%**
- 10s 00f: **80%**

8. In the timeline, drag a selection rectangle across all the keyframes you just created to select them all.

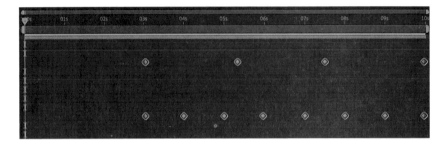

Selected keyframes appear with a blue outline.

9. Choose **Animation** > **Keyframe Assistant** > **Easy Ease** from the application menu to add a bit of easing to the **Position** and **Opacity** changes.

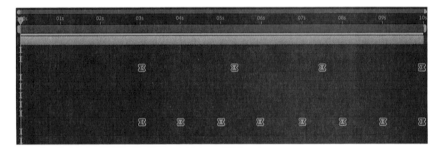

The diamond-shaped keyframes now appear as tiny hourglasses, indicating that an ease has been applied.

The animated elements for this project are now complete. Return the playhead to the start of the timeline and press the spacebar on your keyboard to play the entire composition.

Just as it did before, the camera moves in and shifts to focus on an area, but now there is a short delay before the ghost appears, and once he does, he hovers between the trees as his form fades in and out.

You have created an effective multilayered animation in 3D space using only 2D assets!

Adjusting the 3D Composition Lighting

To add a finishing touch to the composition, you can manipulate the lighting to make it look even more atmospheric. Only 3D layers will be affected by lights you add to the composition, but that's okay because you have marked every layer as a 3D layer.

No lighting

Lighting applied

In this image, you can see how adding just one light can make the animation even spookier. Adding a light and adjusting its properties is simple but has a strong effect on the animated content.

1. Right-click an empty spot in the layers section of the timeline and choose **New** > **Light** from the menu or choose **Layer** > **New** > **Light** from the application menu.

    The **Light Settings** dialog box appears.

2. Adjust the following properties in the **Light Settings** dialog box:

    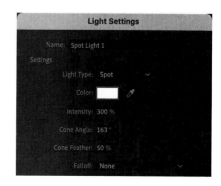

    - Light: **Spot**
    - Color: **white (#FFFFFF)**
    - Intensity: **300%**
    - Cone Angle: **163°**

3. Click **OK** to dismiss the dialog box and create a new light.

    A new layer named *Spot Light 1* that represents the new light is added to the timeline.

    All you need to do now is adjust the **Transform** properties of the light to aim it toward the little ghost.

4. Click the **Properties** toggle > to the left of the *Spot Light 1* layer to open the property groups for the layer.

5. Open the **Transform** group to expose the individual **Transform** properties.

Orientation properties display in the following order: x, y, z. Adjust the three properties to match the following values to adjust the orientation of the spot light:

15.0°, 32.0°, 350°

These changes point the cone of the spotlight toward the ghost. This has the additional effect of cloaking much of the periphery of the woods in darkness and adding further depth and mystery to the overall composition.

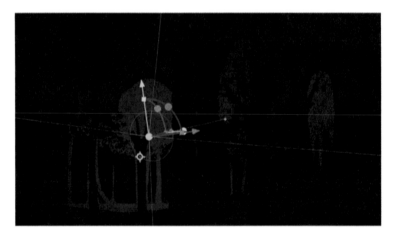

You can also control the Orientation properties by using the 3D gizmo overlay when the *Spot Light 1* layer is selected. If you want, you can make adjustments to the Transform properties and even the Light Options properties to give the overall lighting of the scene your personal touch.

Congratulations! You've created a fully immersive motion composition using basic 2D layers in the 3D composition space of an After Effects project.

NOTE After Effects includes a set of completely new 3D capabilities that allow the use of true 3D models and even more advanced lighting types in this same 3D composition space. We will explore these workflows in Chapter 9.

Exporting Your 3D Composition

Before we close this chapter, let's look at some common options for rendering motion content out of After Effects and into common distributable file formats such as animated GIFs and MP4 videos.

Exporting an Animated GIF

The animated GIF—despite being nearly three decades old—remains a popular format for motion content. You may not expect much out of this file format, restricted as it is to a maximum of 256 colors, yet it can be useful for distribution across several platforms—including the native web.

Let's render the spooky composition to an animated GIF file.

1. With the composition open, make sure the **Timeline** panel is selected and choose **Composition** > **Add to Adobe Media Encoder Queue** from the application menu.

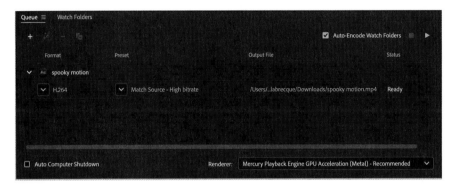

Adobe Media Encoder launches, and the composition appears in the **Queue** panel with a set of choices you can make pertaining to file formats and the render output location. This process sometimes takes a moment or two depending upon your personal configuration, so be patient!

2. Click the selection icon ⌄ to the left of the blue text beneath the **Format** column and change it from H.264 (or whatever the default is for you) to **Animated GIF**.

   This automatically updates the choices in the **Preset** column, as they are based on the chosen **Format**.

3. In the **Preset** column, click the selection icon ⌄ aligned with the preset and choose **Animated GIF (Match Source)**.

4. In the **Output File** column, click the blue text to change either the location on your computer of the rendered output or the name of the file that is to be created.

> **NOTE** When working between After Effects and Media Encoder in this way, a dynamic link will be established between the composition to be rendered and the Media Encoder render queue. The Dynamic Link feature enables you to use After Effects compositions in other Creative Cloud applications without first needing to render an intermediary video file.

If you are happy with the default settings here, you do not need to make any adjustments.

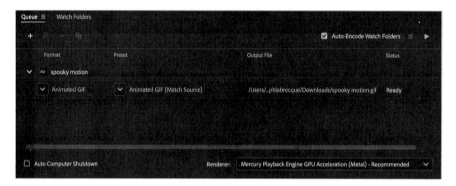

These choices, once processed, create an animated GIF file with no transparency that matches the resolution and FPS (frames per second) values in your linked composition.

NOTE FPS stands for frames per second and represents the frame rate of the composition. Recall that you chose to use a frame rate of 24fps when setting up the original composition. Since an animated GIF is a series of still frames, this means that a 10-second composition will have a file composed of 240 individual frames.

You have one more step to create the file: begin the render process.

5. Click the **Start Queue** button ▶ to begin processing all jobs listed in the **Queue** panel.

You have only a single job queued in this example, but you can add as many as you like before starting the queue.

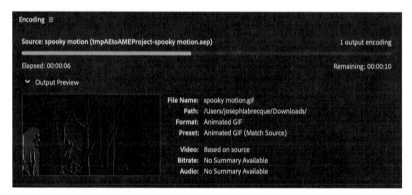

Once the render process begins, the **Encoding** panel displays the progress of the encoding for each file in the queue, providing a preview of the process and even estimating how much time remains.

After the render is completed, your animated GIF file will be in your file system at the location you provided before starting the render process.

Since you used the native resolution and FPS settings from the source composition when exporting your animated GIF, the rendered file will be a rather large GIF. The image shows that my result measures a whopping 37.1 MB for a 10-second animation!

spooky motion.gif
GIF image - 37.1 MB

Customizing the Export Settings

You can get a better result by customizing the Media Encoder export settings before rendering the composition.

With the previous job in the Queue panel completed, you can create a customized set of render settings by duplicating the job and adjusting the settings for the unprocessed item.

1. Select the existing job and click the **Duplicate** button  at the top of the **Queue** panel.

   A duplicate appears with the same settings.

2. Click the blue text detailing either **Format** or **Preset** to launch the **Export Settings** dialog box.

   In this dialog box, you can fine-tune every aspect of your render.

3. From the series of tabbed panels below the **Export Settings** section, choose the **Video** tab if it isn't already active.

The settings that control output resolution and frame rate are located here.

4. In the **Basic Video Settings** area, adjust the **Width**, **Height**, and **Frame Rate** properties to match the following values:

- Width: **600**

- Height: **338**

- Frame Rate: **10**

To enable a change in video resolution, you must deselect the checkbox to the right of those properties or they will inherit this data directly from the source.

5. Click **OK** in the lower right of the window.

The **Export Settings** dialog box closes, and the job in the **Queue** panel reflects the custom changes you've made.

6. Click the **Start Queue** button ▶ to begin processing the new job.

The old job is not processed again, since its status reflects that it has already completed. Only the new job with custom settings is rendered.

Just as before, your customized animated GIF file appears in your file system at the location you provided.

spooky motion adjusted.gif
GIF image - 4.3 MB

With the overall resolution and FPS values reduced, the newly rendered GIF measures only 4.3 MB, compared to 37.1 MB using the default settings. This new result is much better!

7. Quit Media Encoder.

Natively Rendering to a Video File

If you are simply producing video files from your composition, there is no need to use Media Encoder, because After Effects includes a native video rendering engine that produces common video formats like MOV and MP4.

Let's render a common MP4 video file for wide distribution.

1. With the composition you want to render active, choose **Composition** > **Add To Render Queue** to add a new job to the native rendering queue in After Effects.

NOTE MP4 files are the most common video files used across various platforms. These files leverage the H.264 standard codec and can be played back through both hardware and software, depending on the platform. They are highly distributable and offer great compression for a much smaller file size than other formats.

The **Render Queue** panel appears, grouped with your composition timeline, and a new render job is added to it. As with Media Encoder, you can customize many settings through this interface by clicking the selection menu icon to choose a preset, clicking the blue text to open a dialog box, or using an associated selection drop-down.

- **Render Settings:** This section contains After Effects composition-focused settings such as those for quality, resolution, effects rendering, which switches are used in the render from your layers, and so on. Clicking the blue text in this section opens the full Render Settings dialog box.

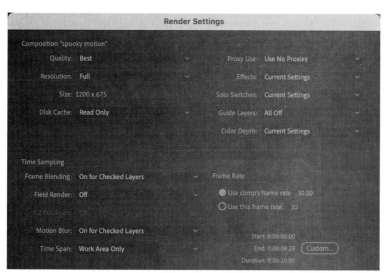

There are also controls for things like frame blending and the application of motion blur, along with the ability to adjust the overall frame rate.

- **Output Module Settings:** While the Render Settings dialog box has more to do with how your composition is translated to a video file and how composition layer settings are considered, this dialog box concerns itself with properties particular to the chosen file format.

  You can change the format here to a predefined set of video file and image sequence formats, adjust audio and video encoding options, and resize or crop your final output.

  Clicking the blue text in this section opens the full Output Module Settings dialog box.

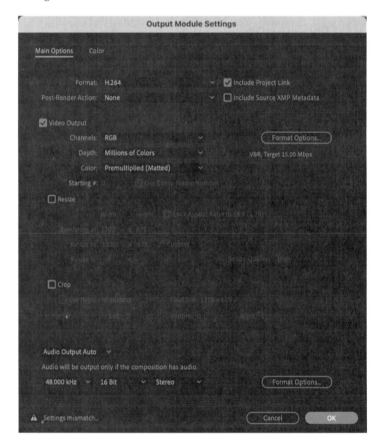

  There is a dedicated Color tab for managing the fine details of how color is translated from your composition to the final render.

- **Log:** The default is to output only errors, but there are options to include additional data associated with the render process.

- **Output To:** This specifies where the resulting MP4 file will be placed following a successful render. Included are several preset locations, but you can click the blue text to specify any location you want.

For the purposes of this exercise, you can leave all settings at their defaults, but if you want to make personal adjustments, feel free to do so.

2. You can always revert to any of the presets for each setting by clicking the icon  to the left of each setting.

I suggest using the following settings:

- Render Settings: **Best Settings**

- Output Module: **H.264 – Match Render Settings – 15 Mbps**

- Log: **Errors Only**

- Output To: **Comp Name**

3. Click the **Render** button 🔲 Render in the upper right of the Render Queue.

The render process begins, displaying a progress bar and associated information for the current render. You can pause or even stop the render entirely with the pair of buttons that appear in the same location that the **Render** button previously appeared.

4. To view the rendered MP4 file, use your system file browser to locate the file in the chosen location.

spooky motion.mp4
MPEG-4 movie - 6 MB

If you chose **Comp Name** as your **Output To** option, the MP4 file will appear alongside the After Effects project file.

In my example, the resulting MP4 file is 6 MB. This is much smaller than the original animated GIF file and only slightly larger than the adjusted GIF with customized settings. The main difference here is that even though the MP4 is only a bit larger than the secondary GIF, you get a much higher-quality result that retains the original resolution, frame rate, and color palette of the actual composition.

This has been a good exploration of using 2D content from Illustrator in a 3D composition in After Effects. However, you are not finished with this software just yet, as there are many more motion-based 3D intersections to explore. Before you do so, you should become familiar with using and customizing 3D models in dedicated Adobe Substance 3D software like Substance 3D Stager and Substance 3D Painter, and even with customized models in augmented reality through Adobe Aero.

Once you become more familiar with the use of real 3D models in Chapters 6 and 7, you will return to After Effects to see how they can be used effectively in that software.

CHAPTER 6

Designing Scenic 3D Environments

We've spent the last handful of chapters exploring 3D integrations within more traditional Adobe Creative Cloud applications like Adobe Photoshop, Adobe Illustrator, and Adobe After Effects. Beginning with this chapter, you are going to resume exploration of native 3D software with an interplay between Adobe Substance 3D Stager and Adobe Substance 3D Painter.

The focus of the explorations in this chapter will be creating a fully realized 3D scene composed of multiple objects with realistic materials.

Exploring Adobe Substance 3D Stager

Substance 3D Stager is part of Substance 3D, which is dedicated to professional 3D workflows and is a separate subscription from Creative Cloud. Recall that we've already had experience in the first two chapters of this book with Substance 3D assets and even certain pieces of software.

Although Substance 3D Sampler and Designer are both dedicated to creating Substance 3D materials, the function of Stager is to use those materials and assets—along with strategically placed 3D models—within a staging environment. A good example of this is a virtual product shoot where you are conceptualizing a product campaign before a studio-based photo shoot—though you can certainly use the photorealistic product renders that Stager produces as your final campaign assets.

Using Adobe Substance 3D Stager, the team had a dozen design concepts ready in less than a week. The Topo Chico launch set a standard for a new way of working, showing that a small, internal team can accomplish results faster with less cost.

Adobe has conducted a number of interesting case studies on the use of Substance 3D Stager for virtual photography. One of the more recent resources hosted on the Adobe website details a Coca-Cola brand case study. You can read more about how the software is used in their concepting work at *https://business.adobe.com/ customer-success-stories/coca-cola-case-study.html*.

Another example would be to create a realistic set of objects for use in augmented reality situations, such as usage in Adobe Aero—which is the direction from which you'll be exploring the use of Substance 3D Stager in this chapter.

NOTE In Chapter 7 you'll use the assets generated in this chapter to explore augmented reality through Adobe Aero.

The Substance 3D Stager Interface

When you launch Substance 3D Stager, you'll see the familiar home screen that allows the creation of new projects and elevates recently open projects for easy access.

Once you click the Create New button, the view will shift to the Design workspace, and an empty project will be created. This workspace is where you will spend most of your time when working in Substance 3D Stager.

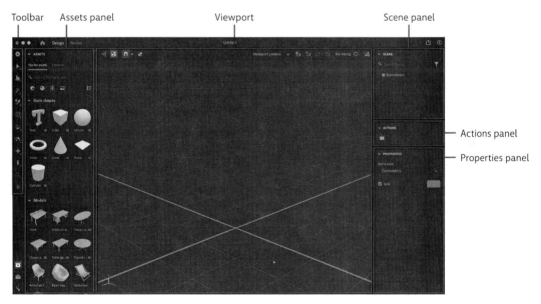

As with any design software, it's a good idea to become familiar with the layout before diving in and creating content. Here are the elements and panels that you should know about before starting work within Substance 3D Stager:

- **Toolbar:** The Stager toolbar contains tools that allow you to interact with the Viewport and the various objects you place within your scene.

- **Assets panel:** This area includes access to various starter assets in the form of models, materials, lights, and images. You can also access assets from Creative Cloud Libraries and other locations from here.

- **Viewport:** This area is the visual center of the software and depicts the appearance of your current scene. You can place models, lights, cameras, and more within the environment as depicted in the scene Viewport. Using the tools accessible from the toolbar, you can interact with these various objects in intuitive ways directly within the Viewport. At the very top of the Viewport, you will also find the Viewport control bar, which you use to control camera, Viewport, and render settings.

- **Scene panel:** This panel functions similarly to the **Layers** panel in other creative applications in that all the various objects in your scene will appear here. This includes the overall environment, cameras, lights, and models placed within the scene.

- **Actions panel:** This is like the quick actions that you may be familiar with from Photoshop, Illustrator, and other Creative Cloud applications. The options presented here are based upon the current selection and provide quick access to common actions for your selection at any time.

- **Properties panel:** The information presented in this panel will shift based upon the current selection. Here, you can access and manipulate the values for certain properties based upon the current selection. Often, there will be a set of tabs you can use to cycle between property categories.

One of the convenient aspects of Substance 3D Stager is that there is a substantial set of starter assets that ship with the software. These assets include 3D models, materials, lights, and images to be freely used within your scenic arrangements.

You are going to use a combination of custom models and materials and starter assets for this project, so let's become more familiar with the **Assets** panel and the starter asset types available.

Exploring the Assets Panel

The **Assets** panel provides access to starter assets and Libraries (Creative Cloud Libraries) through a tabbed interface at the top. Within the Starter Assets tab, you can filter by search terms or by toggling between asset types.

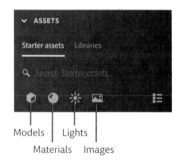

As mentioned, the included assets are organized into four types:

- **Models:** Substance 3D Stager has several model types—standard models exhibit basic geometric configurations, and parametric models go beyond basic geometry to include parameters you can modify through the **Properties** panel to make them appear drastically different.

- **Materials:** You have access to several high-quality parametric materials through the Starter Assets tab. These materials all have standard properties—such as color and roughness—but also include parametric properties specific to that material that can substantially alter the look of the material. You can access all this through the **Properties** panel.

- **Lights:** Three categories of lights are available within the starter assets: Physical lights, Environment stages, and Environment Lights.

    - **Physical lights:** You can place these lights in 3D space as objects and include the choice of Area Light, Spot Light, Point Light, and Directional Light. They can precisely light portions of the scene in very controlled ways.

    - **Environment stages:** This is a special set of staged environments that can have a huge effect on your project. Each works like a preset and includes a parametric panorama, backplates, and a selection of 3D cameras that are automatically created. I suggest staying away from these unless you know what you are doing, since selecting one can have a massive effect upon all aspects of your project.

    - **Environment Lights:** These are parametric images that are applied to the environment itself and are accessible through the **Properties** panel. Lighting is derived from information expressed through these images. We'll take a closer look at this property once you create a new project.

- **Images:** These images can be used as a camera background to your scene. Images can also be applied to models as graphic images for texturing or decals.

Clicking any of the asset type filter icons will display only the selected type and hide the others. For instance, clicking the Materials icon will result in only Materials being accessible within the **Assets** panel.

If you want to view all asset types, simply ensure that none of these filtering icons is activated.

You'll use starter assets later when working with the scenic arrangement project.

TIP Parametric models and materials include the parametric indicator icon in the lower-right corner of their preview thumbnail within the **Assets** panel. If you do not see this icon, you know it is a standard asset without parametric properties.

Working with a New Project

Now that you are somewhat familiar with the interface and various asset types that you can use, let's create a fresh project to work with in this chapter.

1. If you do not yet have an empty project file created, click the **Create New** button from the home screen or choose **File** > **New** from the application menu.

   If you created a new project earlier when exploring the interface, skip to step 2.

2. From the application menu, choose **File** > **Save** to open the Save dialog box.

3. Browse to a location on your local file system that you will remember, and name the file *project.ssg*.

   An *.ssg* file is a Substance 3D Stager project file.

4. Click the **Save** button to save the project and return to your empty project in Substance 3D Stager.

   You now have a new Substance 3D Stager project ready to work with. Note that the **Properties** panel currently shows the project properties, which includes the **Scene Units** options and a **Grid** toggle.

5. In the **Scene** panel, click the **Environment** object.

   It should be the only object currently listed in this panel because every new project includes an environment by default.

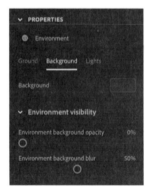

The **Properties** panel switches to display properties that specifically pertain to the environment.

Environment properties are divided into three tabs:

- **Ground:** Allows you to toggle the ground plane on and off and adjust values specific to associated shadow and reflection properties.

- **Background:** Enables the adjustment of the environment background color and visibility properties such as opacity and blur.

- **Lights:** Allows you to toggle global lighting on and off and adjust values for the intensity and rotation of an active global light. Additionally contains environment light properties that are derived from a default panoramic image. You can adjust the intensity and rotation of this light and also choose to assign it a color.

NOTE You can change the image used for your environmental lighting by clicking the thumbnail preview in the Lights tab and browsing for a new image.

Unless you know exactly what Environment properties you may want to change at this point, it is often better to make such adjustments after you have staged some objects within the environment; that way, the results of these adjustments will be much more easily identifiable.

Now that you are now familiar with the interface of Substance 3D Stager and the Environment properties of your project, you are ready to begin staging content.

Adobe Dimension

Substance 3D Stager is similar in appearance and function to another Adobe application: Adobe Dimension. Dimension is a precursor to Substance 3D Stager and is available through a standard Creative Cloud subscription.

Dimension uses an older rendering engine and includes a much smaller set of features when compared to Substance 3D Stager. Generally, however, if you are familiar with one of these applications, you will be comfortable using the other as well.

Although Dimension is still supported and maintained by Adobe, Substance 3D Stager is prioritized with new features and advanced workflows.

Getting Started with Substance 3D Stager

You'll now use Substance 3D Stager to stage 3D models within the environment to create an interesting scenic display. You'll use a variety of models including the architectural column you created in Chapter 4 using Illustrator. You will also explore the use of materials via the mossy stone designed in Chapter 2 using Substance 3D Sampler. It all comes together in Substance 3D Stager!

Designing a Ground Surface

You are going to build a composite cluster of scenic elements with the dual purpose of rendering a high-resolution "photograph" for use in Photoshop and also a set of 3D models that can be placed within an augmented reality space using Aero. To achieve this, you'll use a combination of models and primitives that are available within Substance 3D Stager and also the 3D content you created in Substance 3D Sampler and Illustrator.

The first order of business is to create a grounding element—a bit of stony earth for the column to rest upon.

1. Ensure that the **Assets** panel is visible along the left side of the interface. If it is not, toggle the **Assets** icon located in the lower left—below the toolbar—to activate it, or select **Window** > **Show/Hide Assets** from the application menu.

2. Within the **Assets** panel, in the Starter Assets tab, ensure that you are viewing models by clearing any filters that may be active and click the **Cylinder** shape under the Basic Shapes section.

   A tall cylinder shape is placed in the center of your existing environment.

   You will adjust the object properties so that the cylinder appears shorter and wider than its original form. The cylinder shape will automatically be selected once added to the environment—in the **Scene** panel, the Cylinder object is highlighted, and a multicolored 3D gizmo appears on the cylinder itself.

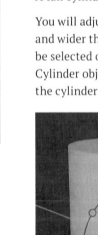

The **Properties** panel will also display properties for the Cylinder object and not the environment.

3. Within the Object tab of the **Properties** panel, adjust the Cylinder properties so that **Radius** has a value of **20** and **Height** has a value of **2**.

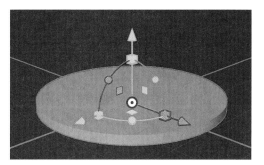

This creates a shorter, wider form for your object.

4. Twirl open the Bevel section of the Object properties and active the **Bevel** toggle switch. This creates a nice, rounded bevel across the Cylinder edges.

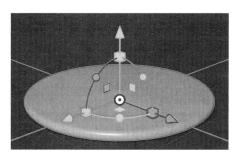

Finally, you'll tweak the placement a bit so that the Cylinder appears to be emerging from the ground plane.

5. Switch to the Transform tab within the **Properties** panel and adjust the **Y Position** value to **–1cm**.

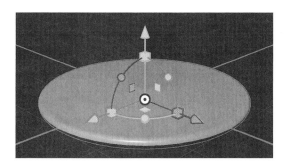

You can also do this by dragging the green cone portion of the gizmo to visually adjust the Y position of the object.

The first object within your scene is formed, and you are ready to apply a material to it. You'll use the Mossy Stones material you designed in Chapter 2 with Substance 3D Sampler.

Using External Materials in Substance 3D Stager

At this point, your Cylinder object has the Default material applied. Most 3D models receive this gray, neutral material when placed within a Substance 3D Stager project.

You could use any of the starter asset materials to replace it with something more realistic, or you can gather materials from repositories like the Substance 3D Assets library on the web. Of course, because you have access to Substance 3D Designer and Substance 3D Sampler, you can create your own materials to use in this project as well.

In Chapter 2, you used Substance 3D Sampler to create a Mossy Stones material by starting with a photograph. This material will work to establish the perfect look to your Cylinder anchoring object for the scene because it gives the appearance of stony ground.

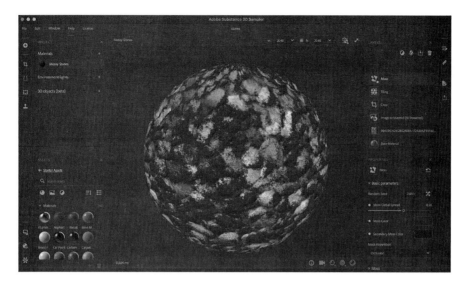

Recall that this material was exported as an *.sbsar* file, which is the distributable Substance 3D material file format. You will use this material on your Cylinder object.

mossy_stones.sbsar

You can find the *mossy_stones.sbsar* file in the exercise files for this chapter.

You'll now import the Mossy Stones material and place it on the cylinder object.

1. Ensure that the Cylinder object is selected. If it is not, click the **Cylinder** in the **Scene** panel to select it.

   A selected object will display the multicolored gizmo overlay.

2. Click the **Add and Import Content** button [+] located at the top of the toolbar and select **Import to Scene** from the options that appear.

   Another overlay appears that lists the import options available. You want to import a material and apply it to the selected model.

3. Choose **Place Material on Selection** to continue.

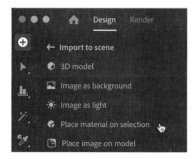

4. Browse your file system, locate *mossy_stones.sbsar*, select it, and click the **Open** button.

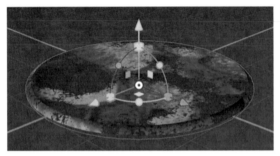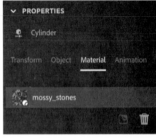

The material is imported and placed on the object, replacing the default material. You can look at the Material tab of the **Properties** panel to confirm this and view the material properties. Additionally, a low-resolution preview of the material appears upon the object.

Depending upon each material used in a project, you will more than likely find that you can adjust the various property values to either customize the materials appearance or make adjustments to the material to make it look more realistic in the overall scene.

As it appears now, the Mossy Stones material looks okay, but the way it is being projected upon the Cylinder object makes the stones appear too large, and the material is rather flat looking as well.

You can make some simple adjustments to fix both of these issues.

5. In the Materials tab of the **Properties** panel, change **Projection** from the default, **UV**, to **Triplanar (local)**. Adjust **Resolution** from **1024px** to **2048px** to increase the perceived quality of the projection.

UV projection workflows are very complex and normally involve creating a particular texture for a unique model. Triplanar projection workflows are more model-agnostic and are projected across 3D planes in place of mapping one-to-one upon a particular surface.

6. Switch to the Object tab of the **Properties** panel and scroll down to locate the **Displacement** toggle. Click the **Displacement** toggle to the active state.

Displacement uses a height map (basically a grayscale bitmap image) to define the higher and lower portions of a texture. Activating the Displacement attribute allows you to render the material across the model's surface in a much more believable manner.

TIP When testing the appearance of your materials, you can (and should!) switch Ray Tracing on from time to time to see how the light and shadows appear in a more realistic fashion. This preview will also be closer to how it appears once rendered. Just be sure not to leave Ray Tracing switched on for too long, as it does take up many more computer resources when running.

The Mossy Stones material is all set. If desired, you can make additional property value changes to tweak the appearance of the material. Recall that when designing this material in Substance 3D Sampler, you were able to expose certain parameters so that they are adjustable in other software—such as Substance 3D Stager! Because of this feature, you can fine-tune the set of moss colors and spread through the Materials tab of the **Properties** panel.

Texturing in Adobe Substance 3D Painter

You could use additional models from the starter assets within Substance 3D Stager and texture them with materials from these assets, but let's use a more customized workflow that involves a set of design software instead.

Recall that in Chapter 4, you used Illustrator to design a custom 3D column that was exported as a 3D model using a variety of file formats.

Not only do you have a model on hand that is a unique creation, but you placed a simple material upon it. Although you could simply import any compatible 3D model into Substance 3D Stager directly, you have a few additional options for texturing the column—that go far beyond what is available in Illustrator or Stager—through the use of Substance 3D Painter.

Painter's role in the Substance 3D Collection is to act as a powerful, detailed texture design tool, allowing you to go wild with materials, brushes, particles, and more. Your fully textured creation can then be easily brought into Substance 3D Stager with these textures intact for immediate staging.

Creating a New Project in Substance 3D Painter

You can use a number of the file formats exported from Illustrator to begin. I will be using the GLTF file, as it is an open standard and includes textures as well.

1. Launch Substance 3D Painter and close the home screen dialog box if it appears.

2. Locate the *Column.gltf* file within your file system browser. It is included in the exercise files for this chapter for your convenience.

3. Drag the GLTF file from your file system browser onto Substance 3D Painter and drop it onto the interface.

   The New Project dialog box appears.

4. Click **OK** to continue.

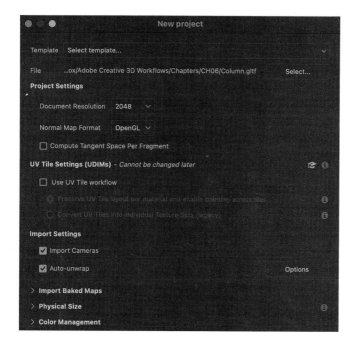

Nothing needs to be adjusted here. Many of these options pertain to specific workflows that are much more complicated than what you are using Painter for, so the defaults are fine.

The 3D model opens within the Substance 3D Painter view along with the material you applied within Illustrator.

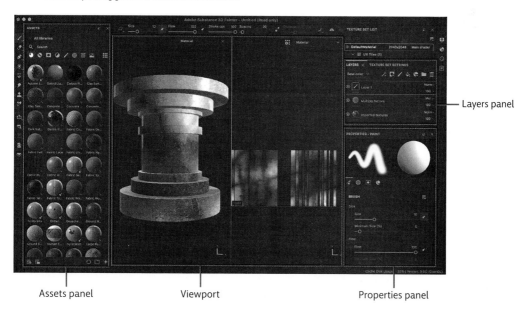

Assets panel   Viewport   Properties panel

The Substance 3D Painter interface can appear rather complicated at first, but if you think of it more like a dedicated brushing tool like Adobe Fresco or even as a sort of "Photoshop for 3D painting," you should recognize certain familiar concepts, tools, and panels.

Probably the most familiar will be the **Layers** panel. Within the **Layers** panel right now, you have three layers that contain information about different aspects of the texture for your model.

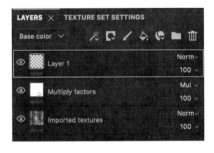

As you paint in additional textures and materials, you will add additional layers to paint upon—just as if using a brush in Photoshop. *Layer 1* is an empty paint layer, ready to receive custom brushwork. The **Properties** panel below it will display properties for selected layers, materials, and brushes as you work.

We can also find an **Assets** panel that is similar to what you had available within Substance 3D Stager. Here you can find a massive library of different brushes, materials, and filters to use to create truly customized textures on your imported model.

TIP If you cannot find the view mode selection menu because your interface is too narrow, press the **F2** key on your keyboard to easily switch to 3D-only mode. In addition, F3 will switch to 2D-only mode and F1 switches to both 2D/3D.

Finally, you have the Viewport, which is a rendering of the 3D model, a 2D texture, or both. You can switch views between 2D, 3D, or both by choosing an option from the view mode selection menu [icon] above the Viewport. I suggest switching to *3D only* for the remainder of your time in Painter, as it is more natural to work with the 3D projection rather than the flattened 2D texture.

Saving a Substance 3D Painter Project

Before moving on, let's save the Substance 3D Painter project.

1. Choose **File** > **Save** from the application menu.

   The Save dialog box appears.

2. Browse to the location on your local computer that you'd like to save the project to and give it a name. I've named my project *columnpaint.spp*. An SPP file is a Substance 3D Painter project file.

3. Click the **Save** button to save the project as a new file.

Now that you've saved your project, you can proceed with texturing the 3D model with a variety of the tools available within Substance 3D Painter.

Applying a Smart Material to the Model

As you have seen, the architectural column already has a texture applied to it because you used a material within Illustrator before exporting it. Substance 3D Painter has a vast array of additional materials within it to select from, so let's locate and apply a higher-quality marble material to the column.

1. Look at the **Assets** panel and enable the Smart Materials filter toggle.

   This will ensure you are browsing only Smart Materials and nothing else.

   You want a marble material, so let's search for one.

2. Enter the word **marble** into the search field.

   Now only Smart Materials that include the word *marble* in their names appear.

3. Using your mouse, drag the material named *Marble Fine White* from the **Assets** panel and over the 3D model within the Viewport.

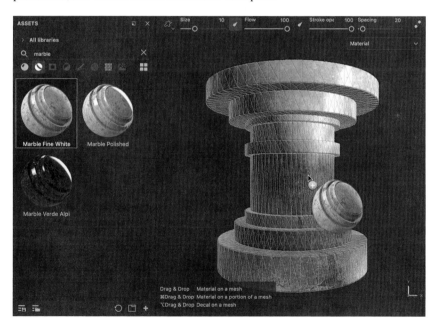

The 3D object mesh is outlined within the Viewport as you hover over it with the selected material.

4. Release the mouse button to apply the Mable Fine White material to the 3D object.

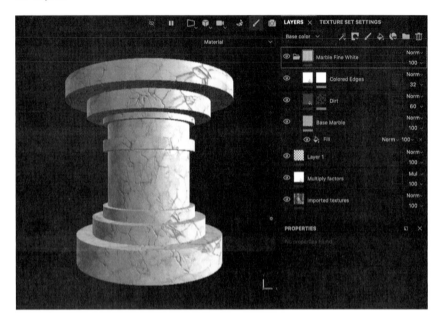

The Marble Fine White material is added to the **Layers** panel as well. Notice that the original layers and associated textures are still in place. Layers above will obscure and overlap layers below—just as when working with layers in Photoshop or Illustrator.

The column now takes on the appearance of the Marble Fine White smart material. In the **Layers** panel, you will see that a folder named *Marble Fine White* has been added to the very top of the layer stack. Clicking the folder icon reveals the individual layers that make up this material.

Painting Details on the Model with Brushes

One of the strengths of Substance 3D Painter is the ability to add materials, generators, and effects to your content with a fine degree of control through the layer stack and associated properties panel. Another massively useful feature is the ability to brush—or paint—various textures on the model directly.

Recall that when you originally brought the 3D model into Painter, you had three layers in the layer stack: *Imported textures, Multiply factors*, and *Layer 1*. The topmost layer, *Layer 1*, is a paint layer created for you to get started fast. When you applied the Fine White Marble smart material to your 3D object, additional layers were added as part of that material.

Paint Layers, Fill Layers, and Folders

When you add a material onto an object, it generally creates a set of additional layers for you to interact with. There are three primary layer types in Substance 3D Painter.

- **Fill layer:** This layer type can accept materials placed upon it. You cannot use the brush tools on a fill layer.

- **Paint layer:** This type enables you to paint upon it using a brush. Generally, these layers must be added manually.

- **Folder:** This type groups layers together in a way like Photoshop. Clicking the folder icon expands or collapses the folder to show or hide the layers nested within.

Layers can also have masks added to them, and all three types exhibit controls for opacity and blend mode assignment. Any effects that are added to a layer will display as indented and below the affected layer within the layer stack.

If you are to brush additional texture details onto the model's surface, you will need a paint layer above the material layers so they are visible. Just as in other design software, layers at the top of the stack obscure layers beneath.

Let's add a new paint layer to the top of the layer stack.

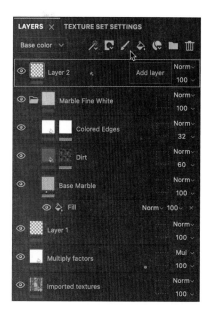

1. Ensure that the folder named *Marble Fine White* is selected by clicking it in the **Layers** panel.

   It highlights with a blue outline.

2. Click the **Add Layer** button at the top of the **Layers** panel.

   A new paint layer named *Layer 2* is added.

   Because you had selected the folder at the very top of the layer stack, the new layer appears immediately above it.

   NOTE You could also simply drag the existing paint layer, *Layer 1*, to the top of the layer stack. The important thing is that you have a paint layer at the top, so anything you do will be visible.
   ---

3. Select the **Paint** tool from the toolbar.

   It may already be selected, as it is the default tool in Painter.

4. In the **Assets** panel, clear the search input and filter only brushes by clicking the **Brushes** toggle ✎ at the top of the panel.

   The **Brushes** toggle appears identical to the Paint tool icon.

5. In the search input field at the top of the **Assets** panel, perform a search for *mold*. Select the **Mold** brush that appears by clicking it so it receives a blue outline.

   Hundreds of brushes are available in the **Assets** panel; performing a search is the easiest way to locate specific brushes.

6. Look at the **Properties** panel to adjust the selected brush properties. In the Brush section, change the **Size** value to **100**. Scroll down to the Material section and change the base color to **#1F3600**—a moldy green.

   The brush preview changes within the **Properties** panel as you adjust the various property values.

7. In the Viewport, hover the brush over the column, clicking and dragging against the various surfaces to paint mold on the column's surfaces.

   As with the orbit, pan, and dolly capabilities you saw in Stager, you will want to at least use some of these view adjustments while brushing across different parts of the column. Holding down the Alt/Option key while dragging across the Viewport will allow you to make such adjustments in Painter.

8. Use your creativity to apply mold to the column in whatever proportion makes sense to you. You can also continue tweaking brush values in the **Properties** panel as you work to add additional variability to your design.

Once you are finished painting mold on the column, it is a good idea to switch from Painting mode to Rendering mode. This will allow you to view a more realistic rendering of your creation within Substance 3D Painter.

9. Choose **Mode** > **Rendering (Iray)** from the application menu to view the column in Rendering mode.

The interface changes as the Rendering mode is engaged. Lighting, shadows, and textures will look more realistic, and an environmental backplate is used as part of this preview.

NOTE Substance 3D Painter's renderer uses NVIDIA Iray—a physically based rendering technology that generates photorealistic imagery. You can learn more about NVIDIA Iray by visiting *www.nvidia.com/en-us/design-visualization/iray/*.

10. Choose **Mode** > **Painting** from the application menu to return to Painting mode.

The 3D column has been retextured using a Smart Material, and you've added additional details to the object by brushing mold across its surfaces. It is ready to bring into Substance 3D Stager and be placed in your scene.

Transferring the Completed Texture Work to Substance 3D Stager

A massive number of export options from Substance 3D Painter are available from the export dialog box. Choose **File** > **Export Textures** from the application menu to review them all, if desired. Although it's good to know such options exist, there is a much simpler way of getting your work into Substance 3D Stager: via the Share menu.

Let's share the Painter work with Stager.

1. Ensure that Substance 3D Stager has been launched and that the *project.ssg* file you've been working on in that application is open.

2. In Substance 3D Painter, click the **Share** menu icon ⬆ in the lower part of the toolbar.

A small menu overlay with two options appears.

3. Choose the **Send to Substance 3D Stager** option from the menu.

This sends the object and material to Stager. Note that the other option sends the texture off to Photoshop for additional work.

NOTE UVs are a coordinate system used in Substance 3D Stager (and other software) that tells the application what part of a 2D image is placed on what part of a 3D model.

In Substance 3D Stager, the Import Settings dialog box opens, allowing you to make decisions around whether to include unused materials in the import and to generate UVs if they are missing. In this case, the settings for this import do not matter.

4. Click the **Import** button.

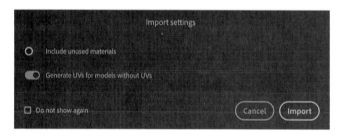

5. The imported column object is listed in the **Scene** panel with the name nodes_0. Double-click the name and rename the object **Column** for clarity.

Initially, the column appears in the center of the Viewport as a very tiny object—far too small for your scene, at 0.12cm.

6. Ensure the column is selected and, in the **Properties** panel, change the **Size** value in the Transform tab to **15cm**.

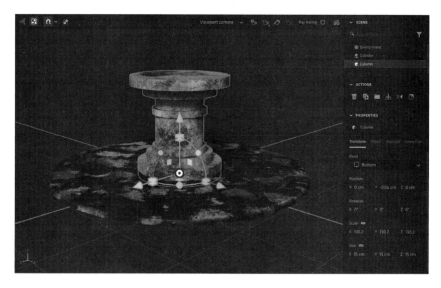

TIP By default, the **Constrain Proportions** toggle 🔗 is engaged, ensuring that adjusting one dimension's Size value adjusts them all equally.

The object now appears much larger than it did when imported. Much better!

7. Using the gizmo overlay or through manipulation of additional transform properties, rotate and position the column object so it appears better integrated in the scene.

I've adjusted my example so the column appears integrated with the mossy stone surface—as though it had been neglected for centuries.

NOTE If you make additional changes in Painter, you will need to import and position your object all over again. There is no round-tripping between Stager and Painter.

The integrations between various Substance 3D Collection applications provide some very interesting—and accessible—ways of working across the different software. This not only provides a fuller sense of control over these workflows but also allows for more expressive, creative procedures when working in 3D.

Completing the Staged Environment

It's now time to wrap up this project by adding a few extra objects to the scene, texturing them with materials, and looking at the options available for rendering and export. This will all be done within Substance 3D Stager, so Painter can be safely closed at this point.

Adding Additional Models

Although the stony surface and textured column look pretty nice right now, you can add a few more objects to tie everything together and improve the realism of the scene. Let's add a few small plants among the stones.

1. Within the **Assets** panel, locate the model named *Tuft Foliage* within the starter assets and click it to add an instance of that object to the scene.

   Note that this particular model is a parametric model—indicated by the parametric indicator icon 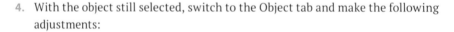 at the bottom right of the thumbnail.

   The Tuft Foliage model is far too large for the scene.

2. If it is not selected automatically, make sure to select it by clicking the **tuft_foliage** object in the **Scene** panel.

3. In the Transform tab of the **Properties** panel, change the **Size X** value to **15cm**.

   Ensure that the **Constrain Proportions** toggle is engaged.

4. With the object still selected, switch to the Object tab and make the following adjustments:

   - Leaf selection: **1**
   - Height: **10**
   - Leaf amount: **8**
   - Leaf bend angle: **8**
   - Leaf scale: **0.2**

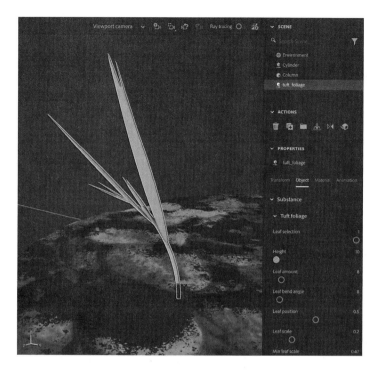

The leaf style changes to a thinner type of leaf, and the entire object will appear to be much more like a tuft of grass than how it originally looked.

There isn't a particular material for leaves within the starter assets, but you can substitute something similar.

5. Filter by Materials and enter the search text **damaged** to locate the Damaged Nylon Webbing material.

6. Click the Damaged Nylon Webbing material thumbnail preview to apply it to the still-selected tuft_foliage object.

7. In the **Actions** panel, click the **Duplicate** icon  to create an exact copy of the tuft_foliage object with all of your adjustments intact.

8. Select the duplicate, named *tuft_foliage 2*, and make additional adjustments to its position, rotation, and various parametric properties to create a truly distinct tuft of grass.

Your scene is now complete and ready to be used elsewhere.

Cameras and Lighting

Although you have not done much with the camera and lighting features of Substance 3D Stager, you can always make adjustments to your scene by using these tools.

- Cameras can be defined from the options above the Viewport. By default, you have a "viewport camera" to work with to use the various camera tools.

- Lights are added from the **Assets** panel. By default, you have your environmental lighting—or else your scene would be completely dark.

At the least, you may want to use the **Orbit** tool 🌀 to make adjustments to the current view before you consider rending the project.

Of course, when exporting for Adobe Aero and augmented reality, the camera and lighting adjustments within Stager do not have any impact upon that experience.

Using the Render Workspace

Although you will be retaining what was created in this chapter as 3D content to be used in augmented reality applications, Substance 3D Stager also includes a robust rendering pipeline for creating photorealistic images based on your assembled scene. This is the primary way of getting content from Stager to applications like Photoshop or Adobe After Effects, so we will touch upon it now.

1. To access the rendering mode of Substance 3D Stager, click the Render tab at the top left of the application interface.

   The workspace switches from Design mode to Render mode.

   From this workspace, you can configure your **Render Settings** and specify **Output Settings** as well.

2. Keep all Render settings at their default and choose **PSD (32 bits/channel)** for the Format under Output Settings. Select a **Save To** location that is easily accessible and that you will remember.

3. Click the **Render** button to begin the render process.

   Depending upon the content of your scene, the Render settings, and the specifications of the computer being used, the rendering process may take some time to complete.

   Upon completion, you will have a 2D, photorealistic rendering of your 3D scene.

4. Click the Design tab to return to the Design workspace.

Exporting for Adobe Aero

In the next chapter, you will be working with the 3D objects within augmented reality workflows using Adobe Aero. The scenic arrangement you have designed here will be used within that particular workflow and so you must export it in a form that Aero will be able to use.

To export your content for use in Aero, take the following actions:

1. Select all objects in the Viewport. You can use the **Select tool** ![select tool] in the Viewport or shift-click all objects within the **Scene** panel to select everything except the environment itself.

2. Choose **File** > **Export** > **Selected for Aero** from the application menu.

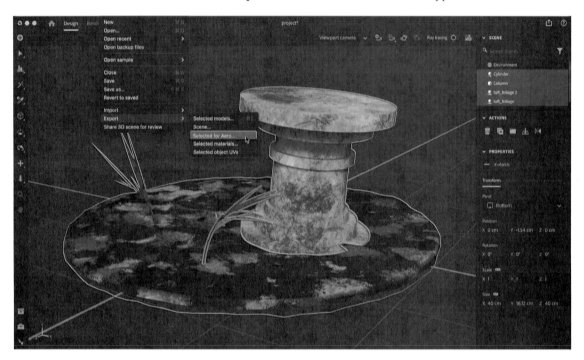

3. An informational dialog box about Adobe Aero may appear. If it does, simply click **OK** to dismiss it.

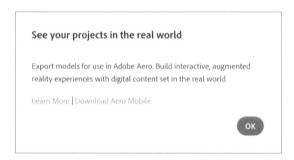

The Export for Aero dialog box appears, and your selection will be converted for use in Aero.

4. Wait until the Ready message appears and click the **Export** button to proceed.

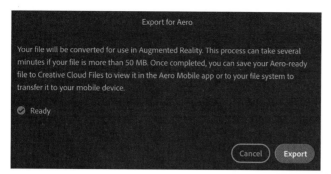

5. Browse to the location you'd like to save the file to and provide a name. I've named my export **ColumnModels**.

6. Click the **Save** button to complete the export process.

The export will be saved as a *.glb* file in the location you specified.

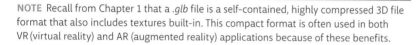

NOTE Recall from Chapter 1 that a *.glb* file is a self-contained, highly compressed 3D file format that also includes textures built-in. This compact format is often used in both VR (virtual reality) and AR (augmented reality) applications because of these benefits.

This file is optimized for use in Adobe Aero and can be easily loaded within that software and combined with additional content. In the next chapter, you will use this file to produce an augmented reality project with Aero.

CHAPTER 7

Placing 3D Assets in Augmented Reality

Everything you've done so far throughout this book has been focused on working with 3D content within traditional software environments. A portion of any modern exploration of 3D software will likely include content using 3D assets in either virtual reality (VR) or augmented reality (AR) spaces. Part of Adobe's 3D pipeline includes Adobe Aero, which is an application aimed at designing augmented reality experiences using content from other software, such as Adobe Substance 3D Stager.

In this chapter, you will design a small interactive augmented reality experience in Adobe Aero that uses the content created in the previous chapter alongside additional assets from a variety of sources.

Creating an Augmented Reality Experience with Adobe Aero

Adobe Aero as a product consists of a unique set of multiplatform software applications within the Adobe ecosystem. Although other applications, such as Adobe Premiere Pro and Adobe Animate, have the capabilities to create virtual reality content—and even interactive VR in the case of Adobe Animate—this is the sole set of applications that deals with AR within this ecosystem.

Adobe Aero is also interesting in that it straddles the line between Adobe Creative Cloud and the Adobe Substance 3D Collection in ways that perhaps no other software—aside from Adobe Dimension—currently does. It is uniquely placed within the overall catalog of design applications offered by Adobe.

The goal of Adobe Aero is to enable the "most intuitive way to build, view, and share robust immersive storytelling experiences in mobile AR," according to Adobe marketing materials. It certainly fulfills that promise with its ease of use and multiplatform capabilities.

Let's see an overview of exactly what you can expect from Adobe Aero, depending on which devices and platforms are available to you.

Adobe Aero Mobile (iOS)

Adobe Aero began as an iOS-only app. No desktop version. No Android viewers. Therefore, this can be considered the primary version of Adobe Aero, although the desktop (beta) is rapidly catching up.

Whether using an iPhone or iPad, Adobe Aero can be installed directly from the Apple App Store—or you can use the Creative Cloud desktop application to send your device a direct link, just as you did for Adobe Capture in Chapter 2. The main benefit of using this mobile version of Adobe Aero is that you can edit the augmented reality layer within an actual environment through the use of the front-facing camera on your device. The drawbacks when using this version of Adobe Aero include having at least one hand occupied by holding the device as you are editing content with the integrated touch controls.

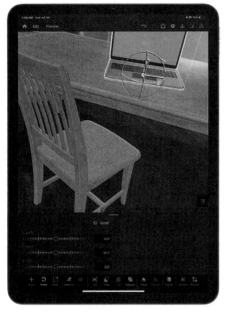

Adobe Aero on iPad   Adobe Aero on iPhone

The controls are all there to define anchors, place and manipulate content, and add interactions and behaviors. They will differ in size and position, depending on the screen real estate and display setting of your device.

For users of Google Android, there is no full version of Adobe Aero available for that platform. However, Android users can view and interact with published Adobe Aero experiences with their devices through a trimmed-down Adobe Aero installation via Android Instant Apps. Users of iOS who do not have Adobe Aero installed can similarly view a published experience via Apple's App Clip feature.

NOTE You can find system requirements for Adobe Adobe Aero mobile at *https://helpx.adobe. com/aero/system-requirements.html.*

Adobe Aero Desktop (Beta)

A more convenient way of accessing Adobe Aero is through the desktop version of the software, available on both Windows and macOS. Still labeled beta software, this version is available to those designers who prefer Google Android to Apple iOS, and it allows for finer control in a more traditional, mouse-and-keyboard interface.

When using Adobe Aero desktop, the major feature that is lost is the immersive front-facing camera view while editing the experience. The benefits are that working with your content is less tiring, as you are working in a traditional design environment with more precise controls.

This is the version of Adobe Aero you will be using to design your project in this chapter—though it is convenient (and recommended) to switch back and forth between desktop and mobile as work progresses, depending on what needs to be done with the content. For example, you will likely want to achieve a proper perspective for scaling and placing content early on. Adding a few pieces of content into the scene using the mobile version of Adobe Aero can set the stage in this regard and provide the confidence needed to continue working with additional objects. Just keep in mind that the same document cannot be opened on both platforms simultaneously. You should always close your project on one device to test or design on another.

NOTE No matter whether you are editing an Adobe Aero project on mobile or desktop, the project will sync across all your devices using cloud documents.

Designing Experiences in Augmented Reality

With an understanding of the overall Adobe Aero ecosystem across mobile and desktop, you will now design an augmented reality experience focusing on the desktop version of the software. Once it's complete, you'll be able to use either the mobile version of Adobe Aero or the lighter, viewer-only apps to experience what you've created within your own AR environment.

Creating a New Adobe Aero Project

When you first launch Adobe Aero, you'll be taken to a home screen very similar in appearance and features to design applications like Photoshop or Illustrator.

The smaller sidebar to the left includes buttons for creating and opening projects, along with access to tutorials and the additional management of Adobe Aero cloud documents. In the large area to the right, you will find a prompt to get started with a new project when on the home screen.

TIP If you click the Your Files tab, you will see all of your existing Adobe Aero files, if you have any.

The first task with any Adobe Aero project is to create a new file to work within.

1. Click **New File** in the upper left of the home screen to begin the process of creating a new project.

   The New Project dialog box appears and allows you to name your project.

2. Enter a project name, such as **ar-project**, in the **Name** field and click **OK**.

   You do not select a location, as all Adobe Aero projects are cloud-based.

The New Project dialog box disappears, and you are taken to the Edit workspace, which is the primary design workspace in Adobe Aero.

Adobe Aero has two workspaces you can access from a set of tabs in the top left of the interface. These represent the Edit and Preview workspaces. The Edit workspace is where you spend most of your time adding content, managing content properties, and generally designing the overall experience.

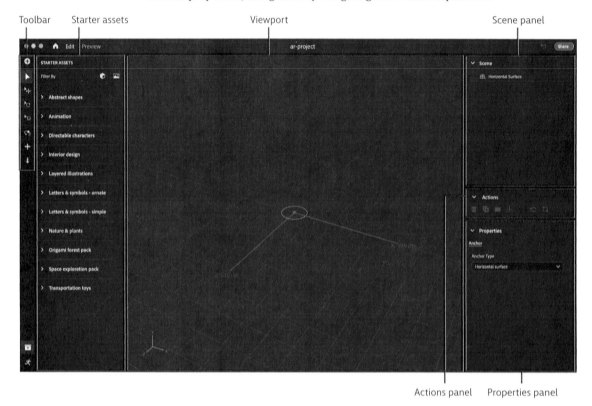

Toolbar   Starter assets   Viewport   Scene panel

Actions panel   Properties panel

Within the Edit workspace, you will find the following areas:

- **Toolbar:** This has tools for selecting objects in the Viewport and manipulating their position, rotation, and scale. You will also find camera tools in the desktop application in lieu of an AR camera view.

- **Starter assets:** This is a set of categorized assets that can be used within the environment. It is similar to some of the more designer-oriented Substance 3D applications.

- **Viewport:** This is where you will place and manipulate various objects to craft the overall AR experience.

- **Scene panel:** This is a listing of all the objects within your experience— including the initial anchor object upon which everything is bound.

- **Actions panel:** Like Quick Actions in more traditional Adobe applications like Photoshop or Illustrator, this panel provides common contextual actions for any selected object.

- **Properties panel:** Once an object is selected, its various properties will be listed here for manipulation.

This covers the Edit workspace. You'll remain in this workspace for most of this chapter.

The Preview workspace, on the other hand, provides you with a large view of your project and a set of navigation controls to simulate the changes that would occur to your view as you move around the environment. It is much easier to preview your content when using a mobile device with a front-facing camera, but the preview feature in desktop does work reasonably well if you understand its limitations.

Importing 3D Content to Adobe Aero

The first thing you will place into your Adobe Aero environment is the architectural column set of models and materials that you designed using Substance 3D Stager in the previous chapter. Recall that at the conclusion of that chapter, you exported your objects as a *.glb* file specifically for use in Adobe Aero. This will be the centerpiece of your AR experience.

To import the *ColumnModels.glb* file that was exported from Stager, perform the following actions:

1. To begin adding content into your Adobe Aero project, click the **Import** icon ⊕ in the upper left. You can also import content by choosing **File** > **Import** from the application menu.

   A file browser appears.

2. In the file browser, locate the file that in Chapter 6 you exported specifically for Adobe Aero. I named the file *ColumnModels.glb*, and you can find it in the exercise files for this book.

3. Select the file and click **Open** to import the *.glb* file into your Adobe Aero project.

   The file is imported at a scale of 1%. Next, you will increase the scale of the imported file so that it appears at a truer-to-life size within the augmented reality environment.

Supported File Formats in Adobe Aero

Although you are going to be using only a few different file formats within the Adobe Aero experience designed in this chapter, the software has the capability of using many additional file formats.

You can see a list of all accepted file formats when working through the import process. In the file browser that appears when importing content, the **Enable** drop-down allows you to filter importable content by file type.

The **All Formats** option is selected by default and enables any file type that Adobe Aero supports to be imported. If you want to be more specific, individual file types can be enabled by changing the drop-down selection.

Here are a few file formats of note:

- **OpenGL Transmission Format:** This allows you to select .glb files as you have done in this current section of the chapter.

- **PSD:** Adobe Photoshop files can be easily used within Adobe Aero—and it even supports layers. You will explore this in the next section.

- **Zip Files:** The zip file format is useful for bundling image sequences from software like Adobe Animate or After Effects to be used as animation within Adobe Aero.

- **Adobe Aero Experiences:** Selecting .real files will enable you to import an existing Adobe Aero project as a unique, new experience no longer tied to the original Adobe Aero project it was exported from. This is one way to share editable Adobe Aero projects with other designers.

Chapter 1 includes an extensive look at different file types used in 3D applications—including many that can be used in Adobe Aero.

4. Ensure that the ColumnModels object is selected in the **Scene** panel and look to the **Properties** panel below it. Adjust the **Scale** of all dimensions (x, y, and z) to **3.3%**.

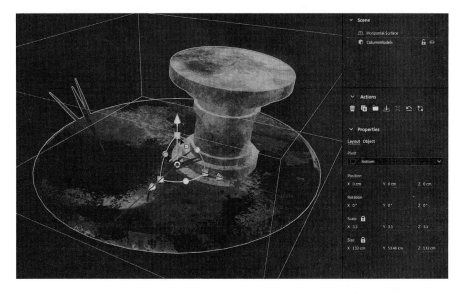

The entire object now appears within the scene at a much larger 132cm in perceived width.

This is a bit over 4 feet in imperial measurements. These measurements can help translate proportions from Adobe Aero desktop to how large they will appear when viewed in the mobile version of Adobe Aero in true AR.

Using Adobe Photoshop Content in Adobe Aero

You can import Photoshop documents into your Adobe Aero experience to create multi-planar designs based upon the layers contained within each document. You are going to use a variant of the textured book you designed in Chapter 2 and bring that into your scene.

Although you can import just about any *.psd* file into an Adobe Aero project, it is best to optimize it first from within Photoshop itself.

1. Locate the file named *book.psd* from the exercise files and open it in Photoshop.

TIP You should be sure the Lock Uniform Scale toggle 🔒 is engaged with any property to ensure that changing the value for a single dimension will affect all three equally.

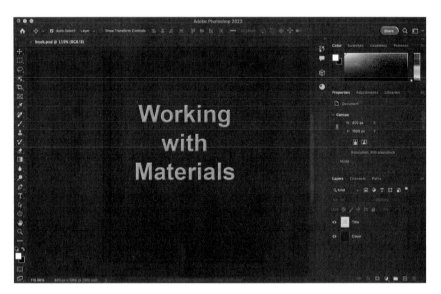

The document differs quite a bit from the resulting *.psd,* as there are only two layers; most layers have been composited together and rasterized for simplicity and for use in Adobe Aero.

2. To export the document specifically for use within Adobe Aero, choose **File** > **Export** > **Export for Aero** from the application menu.

   The Export for Aero dialog box appears.

3. Choose **Preserve Layers** from the options in the dialog box and click **Export**.

   The export dialog box tells you how many layers your document contains. For best results, make sure this number is less than six.

4. In the file browser that appears, determine a location for your exported file and provide a meaningful name. I will name my export *aerobook.psd* to distinguish it from the original version. Click **Save** when ready.

   The Export for Aero dialog box changes to let you know that the Photoshop document is being converted for use in Adobe Aero.

5. Click **OK** to dismiss this dialog box.

   The document is exported as a *.psd* file and is ready to be used within Adobe Aero.

   You might think that since the original file and the exported version are both *.psd* files that the export process is a meaningless extra step. It's true that you may not need to perform **Export for Aero** on every Photoshop document, but if Adobe put all the trouble into this optimization process, why not take advantage of it and be better assured of a compatible result?

Now that you have your *aerobook.psd* file ready to go, let's perform an import to your Adobe Aero project and adjust a few properties to place it nicely within the scene.

6. Switch back to your Adobe Aero project.

7. Click Import ⊕ to open a file browser. You can also import content by choosing **File** > **Import** from the application menu.

8. Browse to your *aerobook.psd* file and click **Open**.

The book is brought into the scene and placed in the center. Notice that the book is far too small and needs some adjustments to its position as well.

9. Make the following adjustments in the Layout tab of the **Properties** panel with the aerobook object still selected:

- Position X: **−5 cm**
- Position Y: **10 cm**
- Position Z: **28 cm**
- Rotation X: **103°**
- Rotation Y: **180°**
- Rotation Z: **170°**
- Scale X/Y/Z: **2.4**
- Layer Spacing Z: **2.4 cm**

These adjustments will place the book on the ground, at the foot of the column.

TIP Use the Orbit, Pan, and Dolly tools in the toolbar to adjust your perspective to better see how your adjustments affect the appearance of your various objects. Keyboard shortcuts to switch across these tools are simply the numbers 1, 2, and 3. These tools will adjust your view during authoring and have no impact on the published AR experience.

Since Layer Spacing along the Z axis was set at −0.01 cm on import, the text layer initially appears behind the textured book cover. Adjusting Layer Spacing along the z axis to a positive number remedies this, and adjusting it to a value of 2.4 cm as you have done here creates a parallax effect because there is now spacing between the layers. You can view the effect of this spacing by adjusting your view with the Orbit, Pan, and Dolly tools.

Multi-layered Photoshop documents can be effectively used to create depth-based art in Adobe Aero with the ability to space layers in this way.

Using Adobe Aero Starter Assets

As you have seen with other software, such as Substance 3D Stager and Substance 3D Sampler, many of the 3D-related applications install with a set of starter assets that make it easy to get started. Adobe Aero also contains a set of starter assets that can be immediately used within a project.

You'll now add an abstract shape to your scene from the starter assets.

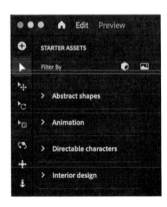

1. Click the **Content** toggle 🔲 below the toolbar to reveal the **Starter Assets** panel. Ensure this panel is visible.

   The **Starter Assets** panel contains categories for a variety of asset types you can use immediately within your project.

2. Twirl open the **Abstract Shapes** category by clicking the small chevron to its left.

This category contains several shapes that vary from the simple to the complex. Some shapes even contain animated sequences within them.

3. Locate and click the shape named **Mobius Strip** to place it in the center of your scene.

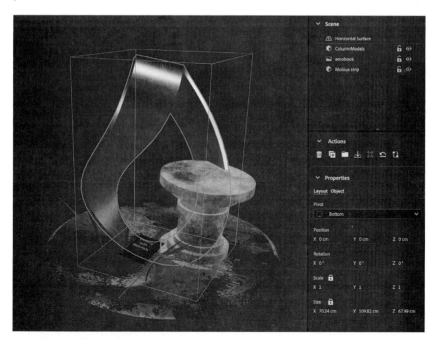

The Mobius Strip shape is rather large and dwarfs the existing content you've already placed within the scene.

4. Use the **Orbit**, **Pan**, and **Dolly** tools to adjust your view as you scale and reposition the Mobius Strip object so that it hovers just above the architectural column. You can also use the **Properties** panel to set the following Layout tab property values:

- Position X: **28 cm**
- Position Y: **56 cm**
- Position Z: **0.72 cm**
- Scale X/Y/Z: **0.4**

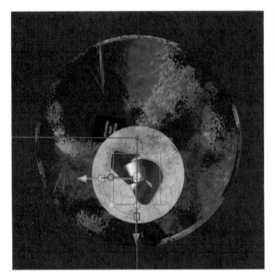

Once you've placed your object into position and scaled it down to appear smaller, if you want to reset your camera view, you can easily do so through the application menu. Simply choose **Camera** > **Reset Camera**.

You can alternatively use the Command/Control+B keyboard shortcut.

Your camera view and perspective will reset to the default. There are also options to **Frame Selection**, which sets the view to contain only selected objects, or to **Frame All**, which sets the view so that all objects that are part of a scene are in view no matter if they are out of bounds of the Viewport frame.

Again, this is an authortime feature in Adobe Aero desktop that allows you to view the experience and its various assets to help with layout and design. It has no impact whatsoever upon how the user viewing the experience through their mobile device will perceive the scene or its contents, as that is all handled via the device front-facing camera.

You now have a nice group of assets within the overall scene:

- The imported collection of objects designed within Substance 3D Stager, from Chapter 6, that uses additional content from Illustrator, Substance 3D Sampler, and Substance 3D Painter.

- A multi-layered variant of your textured Adobe Photoshop book from Chapter 3, set out upon the ground.

- An abstract Mobius Strip object placed within the scene from bundled starter assets.

With everything imported and in place across the scene, the only work you have left to do is to provide interactivity and animation to the experience for even greater immersion.

Adding Interactions to AR Content

If you preview the scene as it's been designed right now, it is still an interesting experience. You can walk around the objects and look closely at the textures and other details. You could leave it as it is and it would be similar to a sculpture at a museum—albeit existing within augmented reality.

To add additional immersive qualities to the experience, Adobe Aero enables behaviors such as animation and interactivity. Although minimized by default, there is a robust Behavior Builder ⚡ that can be activated within the software.

You are going to access the **Behaviors** panel and add a short sequence of interactions and animations to the augmented reality project.

1. Click the **Content** toggle ▣ to minimize the **Starter Assets** panel to allow for more room to work across the Adobe Aero interface.

2. Click the **Behavior Builder** toggle ⚡ that is located just below the Content toggle in the toolbar to activate the **Behaviors** panel.

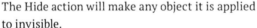

When the **Behaviors** panel opens, it prompts you to add a trigger to begin.

3. Click the **+ Trigger** button to reveal a small overlay menu, and choose the **Start** option to allow actions to begin as soon as the experience starts up.

Triggers determine what sort of events will trigger any actions you want to happen. Triggers are available to run actions automatically at the start of an experience, when the viewer taps certain objects, or when the viewer enters or leaves within a certain proximity to an object.

Beneath the **Scene: Start** trigger indicator in the **Behaviors** panel is a **+ Action** button that enables you to add actions to the trigger.

4. Click this **Action** button and choose the **Hide** option from the menu that appears.

The Hide action will make any object it is applied to invisible.

5. Within the Hide action, choose **Mobius Strip** from the **Subject** drop-down and set **Duration** to **0 s**.

These choices ensure that upon the start of the experience, the Mobius Strip object, which has been placed above the column, will be immediately hidden from view. You will use an additional action to reveal this object to the viewer.

6. Select the **aerobook** object in the **Scene** panel and click the **+ Trigger** button below the **Scene: Start** trigger section in the **Behaviors** panel. Choose the **Tap** option from the menu that appears.

This adds a new section that represents a **Tap** trigger specific to the **aerobook** object.

7. Beneath the **aerobook: Tap** indicator, click the **+ Action** button and choose **Show** from the menu options that appear.

This action reveals a hidden object to the viewer once the aerobook object is tapped.

8. Within the Show action, choose **Mobius Strip** from the **Subject** drop-down and change the **Effect** setting to **Fade**. The additional options are fine at their default values.

Tapping the aerobook object during the experience reveals the previously hidden Mobius Strip object through a 2-second fade in.

9. Let's animate the Mobius Strip object as well. From the same **aerobook: Tap** section, click the **+ Action** button to the direct right of the **Mobius strip: show** action you just added. From the menu that appears, choose the **Rotate** option.

Notice as you work through this exercise that there are quite a few different actions that can be applied to your objects within Adobe Aero. They are all generally added and managed in the same way.

10. Within the Rotate action, ensure that **Mobius Strip** is represented in the **Subject** drop-down and change the **Yaw (Y)** value to **360°**. Adjust the **Duration** to **2 s** and set the **Easing** effect to **Linear**. Select the **Infinite** checkbox to make the rotation repeat forever.

The animation you intend to enable should rotate the Mobius Strip object endlessly at a consistent pace.

Right now, the Show action will activate first, followed by the Rotate action. This means they will be performed in a sequence and not at the same time, which is not quite what we want.

11. To fix this, drag the **Mobius Strip: Rotate** action indicator below the **Mobius Strip: Show** indicator and release the mouse button to stack them together.

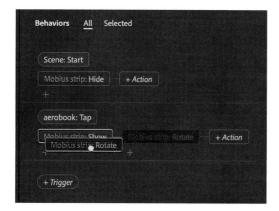

The Show and Rotate actions will now execute simultaneously.

TIP You can also click the tiny plus button 🞣 below an existing action to add a new action to be executed simultaneously in a stack instead of the **+ Action** button that adds new actions in a sequence.

NOTE Two tabs within the **Behaviors** panel allow you to view all behaviors in the project or only the behaviors applied to a selected object. It is useful to switch to the Selected tab when you have an overwhelming number of behaviors represented in the All tab, which is the default view.

You've now completed your behaviors for the entire experience. Upon launch, the Mobius Strip object is immediately hidden while the user explores the experience in augmented reality. If the user taps the aerobook object, the Mobius Strip object fades in and rotates atop the architectural column and remains rotating infinitely as the user continues to explore.

You can see this all laid out within the **Behaviors** panel with the various triggers and actions you've included.

All that's left to do now is share your augmented reality experience with the world!

Sharing an Adobe Aero Experience

Now that you've used Adobe Aero desktop to design an augmented reality experience, it's time to test it and share what you've created. In this section, you'll switch to the mobile Adobe Aero app for testing to confirm everything functions as intended. You'll then export your Adobe Aero experience for others to work on in Adobe Aero and also publish your project to the web, where anyone with the link and compatible hardware will be able to view it in their own environment.

Testing on Mobile

NOTE Keep in mind that the same document cannot be opened on both platforms simultaneously; you should always close your project on one device to test or design on another.

Although Adobe Aero desktop does provide a Preview workspace that you can access from the top left of the application interface (next to the default Edit workspace), the real test is to use Adobe Aero mobile to ensure everything works in your chosen physical environment. Not only is this a useful test, but viewing an Adobe Aero project in a real environment uses the lighting within that environment and renders that directly upon your objects. This makes an Adobe Aero experience very dynamic, as the lighting is adjusted for everyone's unique physical space.

Let's test your project using Adobe Aero mobile for iOS.

1. Launch Adobe Aero.

   When you launch Adobe Aero on iOS, you will be asked to authenticate if you haven't already done so. This allows your projects created on the desktop version to sync automatically with the mobile experience.

   You will first be taken to the Home tab, where you can see any recent projects you've worked on.

2. Locate the *ar-project* file and tap it to launch the experience.

   You will first need to scan the area for a horizontal service and then tap to create a surface anchor that determines where the experience is placed within your physical environment.

   Once you've determined a suitable surface to anchor your project to, you can edit your content directly within Adobe Aero mobile with capabilities that are very similar to those that are available in the desktop version.

3. Click **Preview** ▶ to leave Edit mode and experience the augmented reality project for yourself.

Preview mode allows you to interact with your AR experience just like a viewer would. You can tap objects and run through all the interactions and behaviors you put into place when designing the experience on desktop.

Exporting a REAL File

Although all Adobe Aero projects are saved as cloud-based files, it is possible to export your Adobe Aero project either for backup purposes or to share with other designers. You do so by exporting a *.real* file to your local computer. The *.real* file format is an Adobe Aero Experiences file and when opened within Adobe Aero creates a new project based upon the *.real* file as a cloud-based document.

1. To export a *.real* file from Adobe Aero desktop, choose **File** > **Export** from the application menu.

2. Within the **Save as** dialog box that appears, enter a unique name for the file and browse to any location you would like to save the file to.

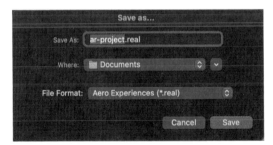

3. Click the **Save** button once you are ready to export your project as a *.real* file.

ar-project.real

The export process completes, and the *.real* file is saved. Your existing cloud-based version of the project remains.

You can then browse to the location you chose to save the exported file to and treat the project like any other authoring file.

Publishing to the Web

To share your carefully designed AR experience with others, it must be published to the web so that a link can be generated for distribution. Anyone with the Adobe Aero app that visits a published link will be able to view it within Adobe Aero, and users who do not have Adobe Aero installed will be prompted to use Apple App Clips, Google Instant Apps, or the Adobe Aero Player (beta), depending upon their device.

To publish your experience from Adobe Aero desktop, ensure the project you want to share is open within the software.

1. In the upper-right corner of the Adobe Aero interface, click **Share** to begin the publishing process.

NOTE Apple App Clips and Google Instant Apps are similar technologies that allow developers to create a "lite" version of the application that can be quickly installed to provide the user with limited functionality. In the case of Aero, they will act like a viewer so the user can launch and interact with an AR experience without having the full version of Aero installed.

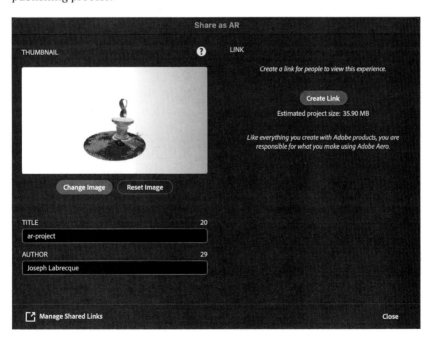

The **Share as AR** dialog box appears. Within the Share as AR dialog box, you can change the preview image that is generated to a custom image.

2. Click the **Change Image** button and modify the **TITLE** and **AUTHOR** fields.

3. Click **Create Link** to publish the project.

Once the project has been published, both a link and QR code image are generated, allowing you to share the experience in different ways.

The link for the published AR experience that you've created can be viewed by visiting *https://adobeaero.app.link/wtR92izq1Bb* on a compatible mobile device. When viewing it in a web browser, you can simply scan the QR code to launch the experience on mobile.

CHAPTER 8

Designing Interactive Projects in Virtual Reality

Following on from explorations of augmented reality projects using Adobe Aero, we'll turn our attention to another way to design mixed reality (XR) projects through virtual reality: Adobe Animate. You can use Animate to design different project types: traditional animations for television and film, digital advertisements, web and mobile games or applications, and, of course, interactive experiences for VR and other use cases.

We'll use Animate to design an interactive 360° virtual reality experience that allows the viewer to travel between different locations by interacting with objects in each scene.

Creating Virtual Reality Experiences with Adobe Animate

When creating an XR design, you can take either the augmented reality (AR) or virtual reality (VR) route. AR projects exist in a real space that you, as the viewer, interact with through some sort of hardware with a camera. Additional content is overlaid across the environment you are in. VR projects are quite different in that they exist in a false environment. They can often be accessed through specialized hardware as well, but VR projects are a bit more accessible because the only hardware you need for many projects is your laptop or mobile device and a web browser.

That is exactly the case with building VR projects in Animate. These projects are very accessible, as they run directly in a web browser using WebGL (Web Graphics Library) technology. WebGL is used for rendering interactive 2D graphics and 3D models in modern web browsers.

Animate is a traditional animation and motion design application with a long history of interactivity. It supports many project types and platforms. Choosing the correct project type is of utmost importance when starting a new project.

When you first launch Animate, a home screen displays with a collection of presets and additional options to create a new project file.

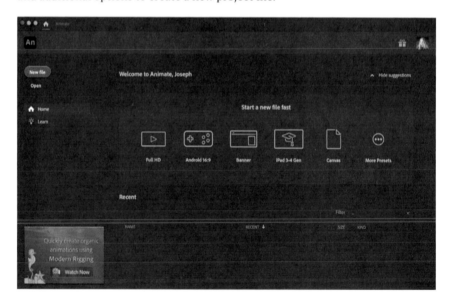

When working with a VR project inside Animate, you have many options for how you put everything together. We'll start at the home screen and in the next section create a new document.

Creating a New Animate Project

To design a virtual reality experience in Animate, you must create your document as one of two VR document types: VR 360 or VR Panorama. Neither is immediately accessible unless you know where to look when creating a new file.

Let's walk through the basics of creating a VR 360 document.

1. From the home screen, click the **New File** button in the upper left.

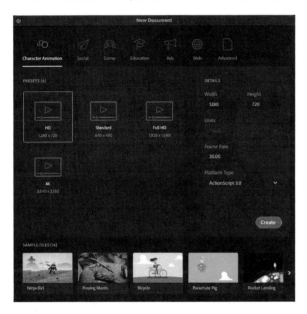

The **New Document** dialog box appears. Categories appear along the top, and each category contains a set of presets.

2. From the preset categories, choose **Advanced**.

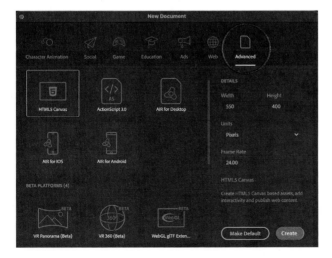

The **Advanced** category is different from the others because it contains platforms and document types inaccessible through any other category.

3. Scroll down until you see the **Beta Platforms** group of presets and select **VR 360 (Beta)**.

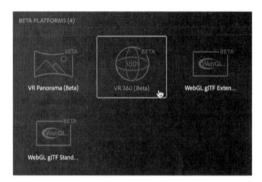

Animate contains a set of document types that Adobe considers to be in beta. Both VR document types are included in this category.

4. In the **Details** column to the right, leave all properties at their default values and click **Create** to create a new VR 360 document.

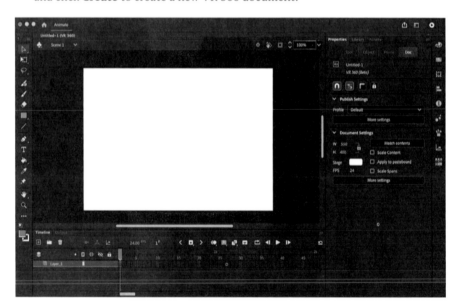

The VR 360 document is created, and you are taken to the Animate workspace.

5. Choose **File** > **Save** from the application menu.

6. Name your file *project.fla* and choose **Animate Document (.fla)** from the **File Format** menu.

7. Click **Save**.

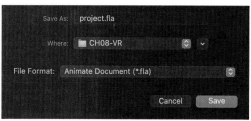

Your project file for this chapter is saved and is ready for you to work on.

The VR 360 document type is used to map equirectangular images onto the inside of a sphere, for a full 360° experience. You, as the viewer, are at the center of the sphere and can look freely in all directions. The following pages explain equirectangular images.

NOTE This chapter explores VR 360. Chapter 10 touches on VR Panorama documents and even includes a bit of VR animation!

Adjusting the Animate Workspace

If your Animate workspace appears different from what you see in this book, here are some simple configuration adjustments for workspace and preferences.

1. Choose **Animate** > **Settings** > **Expert Preferences** on macOS or **Edit** > **Preferences** > **Expert Preferences** on Windows. This activates Expert Settings, which will ensure you are using the Essentials workspace, and adjusts a few additional preferences across the user interface.

2. Choose **Animate** > **Settings** > **Edit Preferences** on macOS or **Edit** > **Preferences** > **Edit Preferences** on Windows. In the **Interface** tab, choose **Darkest** from the Color Theme choices.

That's all! You will be using the Essentials workspace with Expert Settings. The dark interface is really up to you.

Importing Equirectangular Images

You will use two equirectangular image files in this project. Both are in the files for this chapter. They are named *street.jpg* and *inside.jpg*.

One file is a photograph of an external street scene, and the other is that of an internal living space. They look very odd and distorted because of their equirectangular nature.

An *equirectangular image* is a flattened projection of a full 360° view. This is much like how a map of the world can be projected on either a flat paper surface or across a globe. When represented on a flattened surface, distortions occur, especially around the tops and bottoms. When projected on a sphere, however, these distortions are minimized.

NOTE You can create equirectangular images yourself with specialized cameras that are built to do so (such as the popular Insta360 line of cameras) or can use software on a mobile device that guides and tracks you when capturing multiple photographs and then automatically stitches them together to form an equirectangular image (such as Google Street View).

 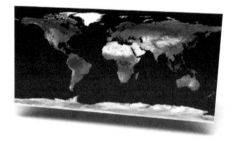

With a VR spherical projection, the content is projected onto the inside of the sphere instead of across its surface.

You will now import both equirectangular images into your Animate VR project library.

NOTE All equirectangular images are created at 2:1 ratio. Notice that both photographs used for this project are 2000 pixels wide and 1000 pixels high to conform to this guideline.

1. Choose **File** > **Import** > **Import to Library** from the application menu to locate and import the two image files.

    A file browse dialog box appears.

2. Select *street.png* and *inside.png* and click **Open**.

    The image files are imported to the project library. Your document in Animate does not change, since the files exist only in the library and not yet visually.

3. Open the **Library** panel (often grouped with the **Properties** panel in the right column). You can also choose **Window** > **Library** from the application menu to access this panel.

    The **Library** panel appears, and both image files should be visible in it. Each file has a small image icon to the left of the filename, indicating it is an image file.

4. Click either file in the **Library** panel.

   An image preview appears at the top of the panel.

With the two images in the project library, you can prepare your project to use the images as scenic background textures in the VR environment.

Working with Scenes

In traditional animations created with Animate, scenes are a way of splitting up the timeline into more manageable chunks of content. They are often used, for example, when the animation shifts from an exterior shot to that of an interior or from a wide shot to a closeup. When designing for VR projects in Animate, you can use scenes to establish an entirely new environment and then write code mechanisms to allow the viewer to travel between scenes.

At the top of your document window is a small label, Scene 1, below the document name tab.

This tells you which scene you are currently working with in a document. You can switch between scenes easily by clicking it and selecting a different scene from the menu. Newly created Animate documents always begin with a single scene named Scene 1.

Your VR project will include two environments: an outdoor street scene and an indoor room. You must create a set of scenes to contain them. You have one scene, Scene 1. Now, you will create another scene and name it and Scene 1 something more meaningful.

1. Choose **Window** > **Scene** from the application menu to open the **Scene** panel.

   This is where all your scenes will appear.

2. Click the **Add Scene** button ⊞ at the bottom of the **Scene** panel.

   The new scene, Scene 2, appears below Scene 1.

3. Double-click each scene's name in the panel and enter the new names as follows to describe what kind of environment they will represent:

   • Change Scene 1 to **Exterior**

   • Change Scene 2 to **Interior**

TIP Unlike with applications such as After Effects or Premiere Pro, when you import images into an Animate project, they exist as embedded content in the project. This makes an FLA file more portable than other project files, but they grow larger in file size with each piece of content that is used.

NOTE Some document types, such as HTML5 Canvas, allow only a single scene to be used in a project. Most other platforms support multiple scenes.

Your renamed scenes help organize the overall project because they describe what content belongs in each scene.

4. Close the **Scene** panel.

You can now switch between the two scenes using the control above the stage.

This allows you to easily switch between scenes as needed. Content that appears in one scene will not be present in another scene unless it is copied there.

You can think of each scene as a brand-new set of layers and timeline, but they share overall document settings and a unified project library.

Adding Texture Wrapping to the Exterior Scene

With your scenes created for this project, it's time to populate them with content.

You'll add one of the previously imported images to each scene to be used as the environment in VR space.

1. Use the scene switcher above the timeline to switch to the **Exterior** scene (if you are not already there).

NOTE The stage in an Animate document is the rectangular canvas in the center of the application interface.

2. From the **Library** panel, locate the asset named *street.jpg* and drag it onto the stage.

The image appears on the stage in the document window. It is obvious that the imported image is much larger than the tiny stage! You can see the black outline of the stage border overlaying the image. The image on the stage remains selected.

3. Switch to the **Properties** panel. In the **Doc** tab, notice that the stage is 550x400, while the image itself is 2000x1000.

You will want the stage size to match the size of the image to be used as a projection.

4. In the **Doc** tab of the **Properties** panel, click the **Match Contents** button in the **Document Settings** section.

The stage width and height are adjusted to 2000x1000, perfectly matching the imported image size. You could have adjusted this manually, but the **Match Contents** button is quick and convenient.

5. Change the view zoom from 100% to **Fit in Window** from the drop-down menu in the upper-right portion of the interface.

This allows you to see the entire stage in the document window. Once you adjust the stage size to fit the image contents, the stage view scales appropriately.

Everything now fits well in the stage, and your view adjusts so you can see the entire stage and background image.

6. In the timeline below the stage, click the *Layer_1* layer and rename it **Background**.

It is a good practice to name your layers appropriately, just as you renamed your scenes.

7. Hover to the right of the layer name to reveal available toggles for the layer.

8. Click the **Create Texture Wrapping** toggle to mark the *Background* layer for texture wrapping.

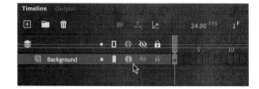

Marking a layer for texture wrapping uses the layer contents as the background of the immersive VR experience when published or previewed. You will not see any changes on the stage, so do not be concerned.

9. Click the **Lock** toggle to the right of the layer name to lock the *Background* layer. This ensures you do not add anything else to the texture wrapping layer by mistake.

It doesn't look very impressive right now because the image remains a flat rectangle across the stage.

Using VR View to Test Your Project

The Animate stage is a flat, 2D surface. The texture-wrapped image is displayed as a flat projection to match. To view it as a 360° experience in Animate, you'll use the VR View panel.

1. Select **Window** > **VR View** from the application menu to display the **VR View** panel.

The view is initially empty and gray.

2. Click **Launch VR View** in the center of the panel to view the projection in VR space.

The selected scene is rendered in the **VR View** panel.

3. Drag the image to change your view in the **VR View** panel and adjust your perspective in the experience.

You can use VR View to easily test your scenes at any time during the authoring experience. It is important to recognize, however, that VR View is not a true test, as interactivity is disabled in this view. For that, you'll need to test in an actual web browser, which you will do a little later.

Let's switch to the other scene and repeat the actions with the alternate image to establish that scene as well.

Adding Texture Wrapping to the Second Scene

The Exterior scene is set up for VR in its own layer set to be used in texture wrapping. Now, you will set up the Interior scene in the same manner using the other image as a background.

The steps you go through are nearly identical to before.

1. Use the scene switcher above the timeline to switch to the **Interior** scene.

2. From the **Library** panel, drag the asset named *inside.jpg* onto the stage.

You already adjusted the stage size to match the previous image, and each image is the same width and height, so the new image easily fits in the bounds of the stage.

Now, you will ensure the image is positioned properly on the stage.

3. In the **Object** tab of the **Properties** panel, select the *inside.jpg* object.

4. Set the **X** and **Y** position values to **0**.

5. In the timeline, double-click the layer name and rename it *Background*.

We need to rename layers across both scenes, because each scene contains its own unique set of layers.

6. Click the **Create Texture Wrapping** toggle to mark the *Background* layer for texture wrapping.

7. As with the other scene, lock the *Background* layer by clicking the **Lock** toggle to the right of the layer name.

This will ensure that you do not add anything else to the texture wrapping layer by mistake.

If desired, you can test your newly created Interior scene in the VR View panel as you did the Exterior scene. You will need to click the Refresh button if the previous test is still open. The Refresh button reloads the scene with your new changes since the last time you used the VR View panel.

Now that the *Background* layer has been marked for texture wrapping, much of the distortion is gone when viewing it using the VR View panel.

Assembling Content in VR Space

You now have a set of two distinct VR scenes established, with equirectangular photographic content serving as the texture-warped background for each. The only differences between the two scenes are the names and images used as the VR background layers.

Creating Portals Between Scenes

Although the two distinct scenes exist as proper VR environments, the viewer is not yet able to travel between them. The viewer should be able to enter a door from the street to visit the interior room and to exit to the street from a door inside.

Not just any type of object in an Animate project can be made interactive. A bitmap image, for instance, cannot be interactive unless it is wrapped in a special container called a *symbol*. Of the three different symbol types in Animate, the one best suited for VR projects is the movie clip symbol.

Included in the files for this chapter is an image of an old, rustic wooden door. The file is named *woodendoor.png*, and you will use it for these next steps.

This wooden door image was generated using Adobe Firefly, a generative artificial intelligence service for text-to-image content creation and much more. The image was then taken into Photoshop to remove the background. The resulting door image was then resized and finally exported as a transparent PNG file.

NOTE We cover Firefly in much more detail in the next chapter. Look forward to it!

Now, you will create a new movie clip symbol to serve as your portal between scenes, using the door image as a base.

1. Create a new layer in the **Interior** scene by clicking the **New Layer** button  at the top of the timeline.

    A new layer appears in the timeline.

2. Choose **File** > **Import** > **Import to Stage** from the application menu to locate the *woodendoor.png* image file.

    A file browse dialog box appears.

3. Select the *woodendoor.png* file and click **Open**.

    The image file is imported to the project library, and an instance is placed on the stage. The imported image remains selected.

4. In the **Object** tab of the **Properties** panel, click the **Convert to Symbol** quick action .

    The **Convert to Symbol** dialog box appears.

5. In the **Convert to Symbol** dialog box, enter **Portal** for the name, and select **Movie Clip** for the type. Click **OK**.

The **Convert to Symbol** dialog box closes.

You now have the Portal movie clip symbol in the project library, and an instance of that symbol exists on the stage where the *woodendoor.png* object once was.

Next, you must position and size the door instance appropriately in the scene.

6. Rename the new layer **Content**.

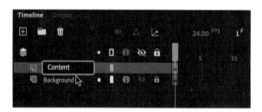

7. Choose the **Free Transform** tool from the toolbar, and position the symbol instance over the existing door in the background.

8. Adjust the position of the instance and scale it appropriately using the free transform handles so that it obscures the original door in the background.

9. Switch to the **Exterior** scene.

10. Click the **New Layer** button ⊞ at the top of the timeline to create a new layer, and name it **Content**.

11. Drag an instance of the **Portal** movie clip symbol from the **Library** panel onto the stage.

12. Click the **Free Transform** tool  to scale and position the new symbol instance in a spot where no door exists.

It doesn't look like it fits perfectly right now, but it will look okay in the VR environment when tested. Try it out; see the "Using VR View to Test Your Project" section earlier in this chapter.

Programming Portal Interactions

With your Portal movie clip symbol instances placed at appropriate spots in each scene, it is now time to program their behavior when they're interacted with in the viewer.

You must first provide names to the door instances so that they can be addressed through JavaScript, which is the programming language used for WebGL content such as our current VR project.

1. Ensure that your Portal door instance is selected, and in the **Object** tab of the **Properties** panel, enter **exterior_door** for the instance name.

You will use this instance name to address a specific object via JavaScript code.

2. Click the **New Layer** button  at the top of the timeline to create a new layer, and name it *Actions*.

In Animate, you can bind code to specific keyframes in specific layers. It is best practice to name such a layer *Actions*.

The only keyframe you have is at frame 1 because you are not including animation across the timeline in this project.

3. Switch to the **Interior** scene.

4. Select the Portal door instance, and in the **Object** tab of the **Properties** panel, enter **interior_door** for the instance name.

Even though you are defining instance names across two different scenes, it is best practice to name them uniquely.

5. Click the **New Layer** button  at the top of the timeline to create a new layer, and name the new layer **Actions**.

This matches the layer structure in the **Exterior** scene.

Each Portal movie clip symbol instance has been given a specific instance name, and an *Actions* layer has been established in each scene to contain the code needed to make each door function.

You will now write the code that enables the viewer to shift from one scene to another by clicking a door.

6. In the **Interior** scene, ensure the *Actions* layer is selected.

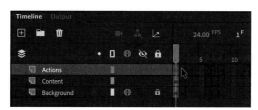

The layer is highlighted.

7. Choose **Window** > **Actions** from the application menu.

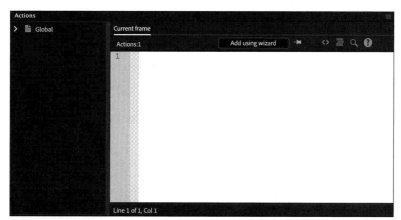

The **Actions** panel appears.

8. Click **Add Using Wizard** above the script window to initiate the Actions Wizard.

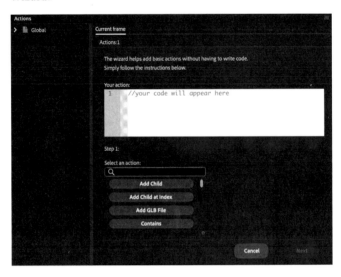

The Actions Wizard enables you to construct code by selecting specific events and actions without having to know JavaScript syntax or the methods and properties of the platform.

Using the Actions Wizard to Create Code for Interactions

Step 1 of the wizard is where you designate the first action.

1. In step 1 of the wizard, search for and select the **Go to Scene** action from the list of available actions.

2. In the code that appears, replace the text prompt in quotes with the name of the scene you want to navigate to—in this case, **Exterior**. You must enter this name exactly as the scene is named, so capitalization matters!

3. Click **Next**.

The Actions Wizard moves to step 2, where you designate a triggering event and the associated object.

4. In step 2 of the Actions Wizard, click **On Click** as the triggering event.

5. From the object list that appears, select **interior_door** as the associated object, which is the instance name you provided to the movie clip symbol instance in this scene.

6. Click **Finish And Add**.

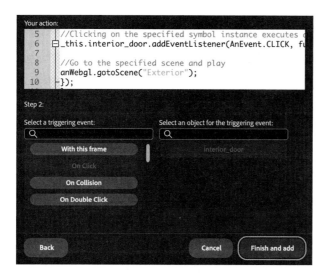

You are taken outside the Actions Wizard, and the assembled code is displayed in the script window.

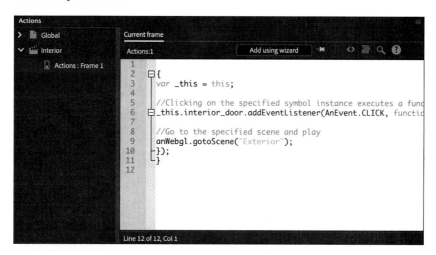

This code instructs the VR project that if a user clicks the **interior_door** symbol instance, go to the scene named **Exterior**.

Duplicating and Reusing Your Code

You will now copy the code from the Actions panel that was created by the wizard and use it in the Exterior scene to program the door.

1. Highlight all the code, right-click it, and choose **Copy** from the menu that appears.

Alternatively, you can highlight the code and press **Command+C** on macOS or **Control+C** on Windows.

2. Switch to the **Exterior** scene.

3. In the **Exterior** scene, ensure the *Actions* layer is selected.

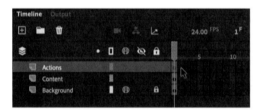

4. If the **Actions** panel is not already open, choose **Window** > **Actions** from the application menu to open it.

5. In the script window, paste the copied code by using the right-click menu or by pressing **Command+V** on macOS or **Control+V** on Windows.

The following is the complete code:

```
{
var _this = this;
//Clicking on the specified symbol instance executes a function.
_this.interior_door.addEventListener(AnEvent.CLICK, function() {
//Go to the specified scene and play
anWebgl.gotoScene("Exterior");
});
}
```

6. Make the following changes in bold to the pasted code:

```
{
var _this = this;
//Clicking on the specified symbol instance executes a function.
_this.exterior_door.addEventListener(AnEvent.CLICK, function() {
//Go to the specified scene and play
anWebgl.gotoScene("Interior");
});
}
```

7. Close the **Actions** panel.

Remember, you must use the exact scene names and instance names for the code to execute correctly! The code to switch between scenes is complete, but you cannot test for VR interactivity in Animate itself. You need to test in a web browser.

Testing in a Web Browser

You'll now view the experience in a web browser to test your code and transport the viewer between scenes.

1. Click the **Test Movie** button ▶ in the upper right of the interface, or choose **Control > Test** from the application menu.

   The project is published and opens in your default web browser. As with the VR View panel, you can click and drag in the scene to view the entire experience.

2. Click each door to transport you into the opposing scene.

This method of testing closely resembles what a viewer would experience once the project is published and served from a website.

NOTE When you test your project in this way, Animate starts up a small local web server (http://127.0.0.1:8090) to get around any security issues in web browsers. You cannot simply open the published files locally and have them function, as it is seen as a security risk. If you want to view your experience from outside Animate, you must host it on a proper web server.

Adding Another Interactive Object

You can add all sorts of files to a VR experience in Animate. A common workflow is to add image files that when clicked provide additional information akin to a museum setting, or even to set up a trail of objects to interact with, as in an escape room.

You'll post a small flyer on the wall that, when clicked, reveals a large version suitable for reading. You'll use the image file *wanted.png* included in the chapter files.

This file is a wanted flyer put together using Adobe Express.

Importing and Preparing the Flyer Image

You'll import this flyer image so you can place it in the Interior scene and add an interaction to it.

1. Switch to the **Interior** scene and ensure the **Content** layer is selected.

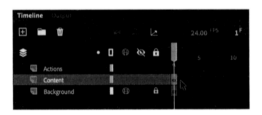

2. Choose **File** > **Import** > **Import to Stage** from the application menu to locate the *wanted.png* image file.

A file browse dialog box appears.

3. Select the *wanted.png* file and click **Open**.

The image appears at the center of the stage and remains selected. It is large and spills beyond the stage bounds.

You do not want to edit the size yet, because you will create a symbol from this at its native resolution and then transform each instance you produce accordingly.

4. In the **Object** tab of the **Properties** panel, click the **Convert to Symbol** quick action .

   The **Convert to Symbol** dialog box appears.

5. In the **Convert to Symbol** dialog box, enter **Wanted** for the name, and select **Movie Clip** for the type.

6. Click **OK**.

The **Convert to Symbol** dialog box closes, and the bitmap on the stage is replaced with a movie clip symbol instance. You can now adjust the size and position of the flyer in the scene.

7. In the **Object** tab of the **Properties** panel, enter **small_flyer** as the instance name.

   An instance name allows you to add triggering events to this instance through code.

8. Choose the **Free Transform** tool 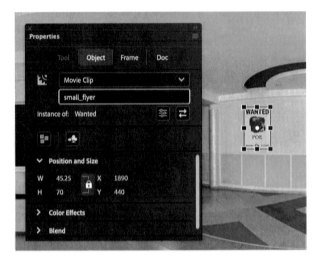 from the toolbar. Use it to scale and position the symbol instance so that it looks as if it is posted on one of the walls of the interior room, like how you handled the placement of doors earlier.

You can also scale and position the poster using the **Properties** panel.

Adding a Second Instance to the Scene

The small flyer is complete. You also need to add the large version to the stage so that its details can be seen when it is interacted with. You'll add a secondary instance to the scene and then scale and position it.

1. From the **Library** panel, drag the Wanted movie clip symbol onto the stage.

2. Adjust the size of the symbol instance so that it fills the scene but does not extend beyond the bounds of the stage. Position it to the right so that it obscures the smaller flyer instance and give it an instance name of **detail_flyer**.

When a viewer clicks the small flyer, the larger one appears.

Using the Actions Wizard to Write Code for Flyer Interactions

The only thing left to do is write the code that makes your flyer interactions function.

1. Select the *Actions* layer in the **Interior** scene.

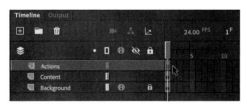

2. Choose **Window > Actions** to open the **Actions** panel, and place your cursor at the very last line after your existing code.

You will write the new code below the existing code that controls the door.

3. Click the **Add Using Wizard** button above the script editor.

4. For step 1 of the wizard, select the action named **Set Visibility** from the list of actions. To find it more easily, you can use the search input above the list.

5. For the target object, choose **detail_flyer** from the list of instance names that appears.

   The following code appears in the editor before the steps:

   ```
   _this.detail_flyer.visible = true;
   ```

6. In the code editor, change the value from `true` to **false** so that the line of code reads `_this.detail_flyer.visible = false;`.

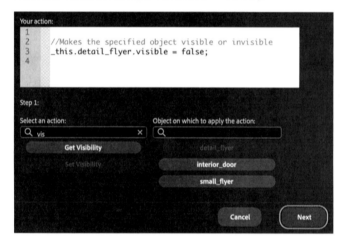

   This renders the detail_flyer instance invisible when the VR project launches.

7. Click **Next**.

8. In step 2, select **With This Frame** as the triggering event, and click **Finish And Add**.

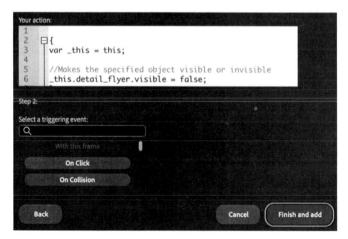

The Actions Wizard returns to the script editor and displays your code as follows:

```
{
var _this = this;
//Makes the specified object visible or invisible
_this.detail_flyer.visible = false;
}
```

Using **With This Frame** as a triggering event means that the instance will be set to invisible as soon as the playhead reaches this frame. You have only one frame in your timeline, which means it will happen immediately.

9. Click the **Test Movie** button  or choose **Control** > **Test** from the application menu to test the code in a web browser.

NOTE You must test the interactivity of the code in a web browser. The VR View panel will not process the code in any way.

10. Visit the interior by passing through the portal on the street. Look around the interior room. The larger version of the flyer never appears because you have hidden it with code.

Writing Interaction Code by Hand

You have now used the Actions Wizard enough that you can likely piece together the remainder of the code by hand. You have code that performs some event based on a click by the user, and you know the property that you can set to make objects visible or invisible.

TIP Writing code in this way and modifying examples to suit different scenarios is a great way to learn how to code in just about any environment.

To complete the interactions, you must set a click event on the small flyer that will change the visibility of the larger version and then add a click event to the large version that turns it invisible when clicked.

Let's write some code!

1. In the **Actions** panel, copy the first piece of code that you wrote with the wizard (to handle the door) by highlighting it and pressing **Command+C** on macOS or **Control+C** on Windows.

2. Place your cursor beneath the second piece of code, press **Enter** or **Return** to create a new line, and paste the copied code by pressing **Command+V** on macOS or **Control+V** on Windows.

   The pasted code block should look like this:

   ```
   {
   var _this = this;
   //Clicking on the specified symbol instance executes a function.
   _this.interior_door.addEventListener(AnEvent.CLICK, function() {
   //Go to the specified scene and play
   anWebgl.gotoScene("Exterior");
   });
   }
   ```

3. Change the code so that the click event targets the **small_flyer** instance instead of the **interior_door** instance:

   ```
   this.small_flyer.addEventListener(AnEvent.CLICK, function() {
   ```

4. Delete the entire line of code that switches scenes:

   ```
   anWebgl.gotoScene("Exterior");
   ```

5. Replace the line you removed with the following line of code:

   ```
   this.detail_flyer.visible = true;
   ```

   The resulting block of code will look like this (the code comments are omitted for clarity):

   ```
   {
   var _this = this;
   _this.small_flyer.addEventListener(AnEvent.CLICK, function() {
   _this.detail_flyer.visible = true;
   });
   }
   ```

6. Copy the chunk of code you just modified and paste it after the existing code. You will now modify this code block to add a click event to the large flyer to close it.

7. Change the code to bind the click event to **i**, and change the `visible` property of **detail_flyer** to **false** to hide the large flyer once it is clicked.

```
{
var _this = this;
_this.detail_flyer.addEventListener(AnEvent.CLICK, function() {
_this.detail_flyer.visible = false;
});
}
```

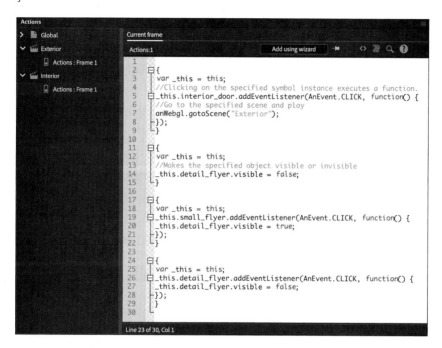

The full, final code for the **Interior** scene is as follows. Comments have been omitted for clarity:

```
{
var _this = this;
_this.interior_door.addEventListener(AnEvent.CLICK, function() {
anWebgl.gotoScene("Exterior");
});
}

{
var _this = this;
_this.detail_flyer.visible = false;
}
```

```
{
var _this = this;
_this.small_flyer.addEventListener(AnEvent.CLICK, function() {
_this.detail_flyer.visible = true;
});
}

{
var _this = this;
_this.detail_flyer.addEventListener(AnEvent.CLICK, function() {
_this.detail_flyer.visible = false;
});
}
```

NOTE Even one tiny
mistake in the code can
render the entire expe-
rience unfunctional. If
that happens to you,
double-check your
code against what you
see in this book.

The code includes click event triggers on three symbol instances: the door, the small version of the flyer, and the larger version of the flyer. Additionally, you set the large version to be hidden upon the start of the VR experience.

8. Test your VR experience in a web browser.

You can move from the exterior into the interior. Once there, you can locate and click the small flyer to reveal the larger version. When you click the large version, it closes.

Working with 3D Objects

In this chapter, you have explored how to import image files, convert them to symbols, and add interactions to them. One of the neat things about WebGL is that it supports true 3D models as well.

In addition to the completed VR project, I thought it would be fun to add a 3D model into the experience to demonstrate this feature. While we won't be doing much with this model aside from importing it—as that involves a lot of code and is beyond the scope of this book—I hope it gives you ideas for experimenting with some of the advanced WebGL and VR capabilities of Animate!

I've prepared a 3D model of Earth represented as a globe; it's based on a public domain image distributed by NASA. You may recall seeing an image of this asset at the beginning of this chapter.

This model was created in Adobe Substance 3D Stager with a simple sphere mesh and the NASA "Blue Marble 2002" image mapped across its surface as a decal graphic.

Let's get a bit surreal and include this 3D model in your VR project.

1. Since this object will be part of the visual content of the project, select the **Content** layer in the **Exterior** scene.

2. Choose **File > Import > Import to Stage** from the application menu to locate the *BlueMarble2002.glb* 3D model file.

3. Click **Open**.

The file is placed at the center of the stage, but all that is visible is a place-holder. The stage lacks the ability to render 3D models.

However, testing in the VR View panel or through a web browser will render these file types correctly.

4. Launch the project in the **VR View** panel to see the 3D model rendered in your VR project. Remember to click the **Refresh** button to see your changes!

The "blue marble" hovers in the VR street view. Weird!

You can control the size, rotation, position, and more aspects of 3D models with code. The following URL lists some common properties you may want to adjust through the Actions panel along with the code to do so: *https://helpx.adobe.com/ animate/using/virtual-reality.html.*

Of course, you can also use the Actions Wizard to adjust properties.

Publishing VR Projects

When publishing your virtual reality creation, it is a good idea to review the settings for a WebGL VR project. There are some choices to make regarding how things are published, and you will likely want to choose a specific name and location for the published files.

1. In the **Doc** tab of the **Properties** panel, click **More Settings** in the **Publish Settings** section.

   The **Publish Settings** dialog box appears.

2. In the **Publish Settings** dialog box, choose a name and location for your published files.

You can make additional choices regarding the published image resolution, whether the timeline loops or not, whether hidden layers should be included, and whether to use code libraries hosted in the cloud.

3. Click **Publish** to publish your VR project.

4. Click **OK** to dismiss the dialog box.

5. Locate the bundle of files that were published in the location you chose.

You will find an HTML file along with a folder filled with various assets and code.

Remember that the bundle of files that is produced when you publish must be served from either a local or remote web server. Simply clicking the resulting HTML file will not run the project, due to browser security restrictions.

CHAPTER 9

Manipulating 3D Models for Motion Graphic Designs

In this chapter, we return to Substance 3D Stager and Adobe After Effects for a different approach. We'll be designing the 3D model of a product in Substance 3D Stager with assets created in Adobe Illustrator and Adobe Express. We'll use this 3D model in an After Effects composition alongside additional 3D and 2D content using the new Advanced 3D rendering engine.

We'll also explore the creation of background elements for the composition through generative AI and Adobe Firefly, see how to work with 3D text elements, and use advanced lighting techniques through HDRi imagery. A lot of workflows, techniques, and software converge in this chapter!

Designing Motion Content with 3D Models

In Chapter 5's introduction to 3D in After Effects, we looked at two ways of working in 3D space. The first was through the manipulation of flat graphics in perspective to give the appearance of 3D, and the second was to use actual 3D models. After Effects is capable of dealing with both methods within the same composition.

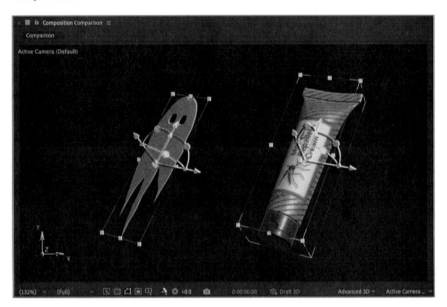

In this figure, you can see that After Effects shows both the 2D object and the 3D object as 3D layers in a single composition. Their appearance and the related controls inform you of their nature. The 2D object, when selected, exhibits a flat transformation rectangle around it, whereas the 3D object appears as though contained in a three-dimensional transformation cube. This difference is the projected volume of the object in 3D space.

This chapter focuses on native support for true 3D models and other aspects of the Advanced 3D render engine.

Exploring the Advanced 3D Render Engine

When you create a new composition, After Effects provides three choices of 3D rendering engine in the 3D Renderer tab of the Composition Settings dialog box.

1. Choose **Composition** > **New Composition** from the application menu to access this dialog box as part of the composition creation workflow, or choose **Composition** > **Composition Settings** with an existing composition selected.

   Three tabs are available to you in this dialog box: **Basic**, **Advanced**, and **3D Renderer**.

2. Choose **3D Renderer** to select the rendering engine you'd like to use and to see the features that are supported by each engine.

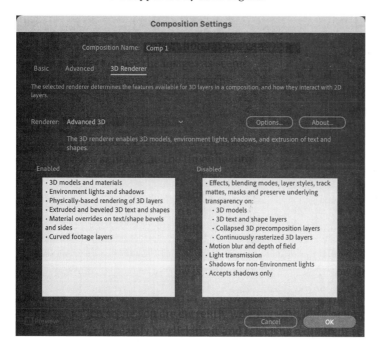

Beginning with the release of Adobe After Effects 2024 (version 24.2), the following engines are available:

- **Classic 3D:** The default rendering engine before the Advanced 3D engine became available. This renderer enables your 2D layers to be positioned in 3D space.

- **Advanced 3D:** This rendering engine, which is the focus of this chapter, is new to After Effects after a long gestation in the public beta. When Advanced 3D is selected, you can use true 3D models and materials, environmental lighting and shadows, extruded shape and text content, and more advanced 3D workflows.

- **Cinema 4D:** This rendering engine functions alongside the Cinema 4D Lite software application, which you can optionally install. This rendering engine enables the extrusion of shape and text elements.

In this chapter, you will use **Advanced 3D** as the 3D renderer. This is the default rendering engine, and it is automatically activated when creating a 3D layer or importing a 3D model.

3. Click the **Options** button on the **3D Renderer** tab of the Composition Settings dialog box. The **Advanced 3D Render Options** dialog box displays.

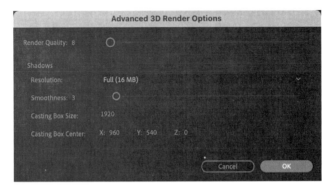

From here, you can fine-tune the render performance for your hardware and project. The following properties are available:

- **Render Quality:** A lower setting for this property makes editing your composition easier, while a higher value represents a greater degree of quality as you work.

  You can set it from 1 to 300 with the associated slider control.

- **Shadows Resolution:** The higher the MB value this is set to, the more realistic the shadows cast upon your 3D content will appear.

  You can choose values of Half (2 MB), Full (16 MB), or Double (128 MB) from the drop-down.

- **Shadows Smoothness:** The Smoothness property works alongside Render Quality and indicates how smooth the shadows appear as they are generated. A high setting can negatively affect performance while you work in the composition but will give smoother results.

  Set this from 1 to 32 with the slider.

- **Shadows Casting Box Size:** The casting box determines the area within which shadows are produced in your composition. Keeping this size only as large as needed will keep things from being too laggy, as it would be pointless to cast shadows in areas that are not visible, for example.

- **Shadows Casting Box Center:** The casting box size is measured from this center point. Since you are working in 3D space, you must set the center across all three dimensions: X, Y, and Z.

- **Fit to Scene:** This button will automatically set the Casting Box Size and Casting Box Center properties to match your composition content.

  Only content capable of casting shadows is considered.

You can alternatively access the **Advanced 3D Render Options** dialog box from below the composition panel. Click the **3D Renderer** drop-down and choose the **Renderer Options** list item.

This provides quicker access to make adjustments as you work, since it displays the dialog box immediately.

TIP You can also switch between 3D rendering engines from this same drop-down, but this is a choice that should be made early on. You usually would not switch the 3D renderer in the middle of working on a composition.

Exploring the Major Features of the Advanced 3D Renderer

Now that you are familiar with how to activate the Advanced 3D renderer and tweak the options to your liking, let's look at the major features enabled by this rendering engine in After Effects.

3D Model Support

One of the most important features of the new rendering engine is the ability to work with true 3D models in a composition. After Effects supports the GLB and GLTF formats for import and use in any composition using the Advanced 3D render engine.

GLB and GLTF are highly popular file formats and include not only the 3D meshes that form a model but also any materials and images placed on them.

HDRi Image-Based Lighting

High dynamic range imaging (HDRi) files are generally shot as equirectangular images and include extra information regarding lighting due to how HDR images are created. Using HDRi imagery in a composition enables you to use this lighting information as the source for environmental lights that have a direct effect on 3D layers and how they are lit in a scene.[1]

---

1. Image sourced from *https://hdri-haven.com/hdri/abandoned-cemetary*

You can gather HDRi images from several sources, including the Substance 3D Assets Collection or Adobe Stock (see Chapter 1). The image file in this figure was gathered from HDRI-HAVEN, which is a resource dedicated to making free, high-quality HDRi images available to 3D artists.

Camera and Light Extraction

Not only can GLB and GLTF files contain 3D models and related materials, but they can also hold information regarding cameras and lights. These cameras and lights can be extracted from imported 3D files of this kind and used as cameras and lights in a composition.

To extract any lights that are present in a 3D model in your composition, select the layer with the 3D model and choose **Layer** > **Light** > **Create Lights from 3D Model** from the application menu.

To extract any cameras that are present in a 3D model in your composition, select the layer with the 3D model and choose **Layer** > **Camera** > **Create Cameras from 3D Model** from the application menu.

If the extracted lights and cameras include animation, keyframes will be placed on the timeline.

2D/3D Effect Workflows

It's important to remember that you can combine 2D and 3D layers in the same composition. The Advanced 3D rendering engine enables effects that reference other layers to mingle across 2D and 3D space. This allows effects such as Displacement Map, Vector Blur, or Calculations to use a 3D model layer as a source to create highly stylized renders.

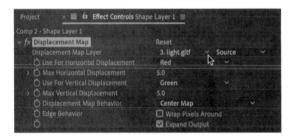

We'll explore much of this new Advanced 3D rendering feature set in the remainder of this chapter, but first let's design a 3D model in Substance 3D Stager for the composition.

Designing a 3D Product for Motion Design

Before you venture back into After Effects to explore the new Advanced 3D render engine, you'll need access to a suitable 3D model to work with. As you saw in Chapter 6, you can use Substance 3D Stager to design models and export them in many different file formats, some of which can be used in an After Effects composition.

Creating a New Project

Launch Substance 3D Stager and create a new file to design a simple 3D model for export. You'll use starter assets and a few custom decorative elements to form and brand the mesh.

Let's create a new project to work with.

1. Click **Create New** on the home screen or choose **File** > **New** from the application menu.

This creates a fresh Substance 3D Stager project.

2. From the application menu, choose **File** > **Save** to display the **Save As** dialog box.

3. Browse to a location on your local file system that you will remember and name the file *mosquito.ssg*.

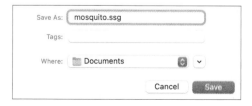

4. Click **Save** to save the project and return to your empty scene in Substance 3D Stager.

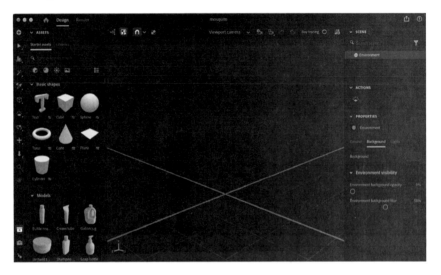

You now have an empty Substance 3D Stager project ready to work with. This environment exists only for your 3D model design and export, so don't be concerned about the environment or camera properties, since you will be exporting the model along with any applied design elements and not rendering the content.

Designing a Branded Product

Now that you have a clean project to work in, you need to identify a 3D model and then apply a set of chosen materials to it for greater realism.

1. Ensure that the **Assets** panel is activated and visible along the left side of the Substance 3D Stager interface. If it is not, click the **Assets** button ▣ in the lower left of the interface to activate it.

   Next, you will choose a 3D model and select appropriate materials to place on the various mesh parts that form the model.

2. In the **Starter Assets** tab of the **Assets** panel, type **tube** in the search field at the top to display any assets that contain "tube" in their name.

   If you do not see any models appear, be sure none of the filters below the search field are active.

3. Click the **Cream tube** model from the set of assets that appear.

The tube is added to the very center of your environment and appears as an entry in the **Scene** panel.

4. In the **Scene** panel, open the **cream_tube** mesh group to reveal the individual mesh parts that compose the model.

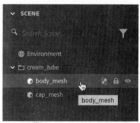

One mesh represents the tube body, and the other represents the tube cap. Each mesh can have its properties adjusted independently of the other.

NOTE Each part of the cream_tube group is brought into the project with a set of simple default materials applied. The meshes must have these plain materials at this stage so that you can visualize the actual model—much like how paths in Illustrator must have some sort of appearance properties to visualize them when they're not selected.

---

5. In the **cream_tube** group, select the **body_mesh** object.

The **body_mesh** object is highlighted in the **Scene** panel, indicating that it is now selected.

Additionally, the visual model part in the environment exhibits a blue outline, and the **Properties** panel changes to display properties specific to the selected object.

The tube body includes a boring gray default material that you will change to something more realistic and interesting.

6. In the **Starter Assets** tab, search for the term **plastic** to display several materials.

Many starter assets are meant to exhibit the look of plastic in some way. Quite a lot of choices!

7. Scroll through the materials and locate the **Shinny Plastic** material. It appears as a reflective, deep orange material with subtle creases.

8. Click the material preview to apply it to the selected **body_mesh** object.

   Notice that since only the **body_mesh** object was selected, the Shinny Plastic material is applied to that individual part of the overall model group. If the entire group were selected, the **cap_mesh** object would take on this appearance as well.

9. Select the **cap_mesh** object in the **Scene** panel.

10. In the Starter Assets tab, click the **Hard Plastic** material to apply it to the cap of the tube.

    Since you did not change or clear out the previous search for "plastic," you did not need to perform a fresh search.

The Hard Plastic material is applied to the **cap_mesh** object.

Adjusting Material Properties

You could leave these materials at their default appearance, of course, but the tube is a bit too orange for the overall design. To finish working with these materials, you will adjust the color of the Shinny Plastic material.

1. In the **Scene** panel, select the **body_mesh** object again and look at the **Properties** panel.

2. Click the **Material** tab in the **Properties** panel and ensure the **Shinny Plastic** material is selected to view the properties that you can adjust.

   Many, many properties can be adjusted, and they differ greatly from material to material.

3. Scroll down in the **Shinny Plastic** section of the **Substance** properties until you locate the **Color** property, and then click it to display the color picker overlay. Adjust the color to more yellow and less orange.

I am using the value **#C5870D**, which can be entered into the **Hex** input box in the color picker overlay.

NOTE If you do not see Hex as your unit type in the color picker overlay, click the displayed unit type to select it from the drop-down. Available types are RGB, HSL, HSV, HWB, CMYK, and Hex.

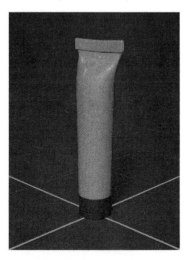

With individual materials chosen, applied, and adjusted, the basic design for the cream tube model is complete.

It already looks very realistic with the softer, creased look of the tube body and the harder, duller appearance of the plastic cap. Applying a set of visually distinctive materials to a model in this way is a great method of achieving a realistic look for your design.

Applying Branding Assets to the Design

To complete the cream tube design, you will include specific branding assets in the After Effects composition. These branding assets include a pattern and a label.

The exercise files for this chapter include a file named *pattern.png*. You will apply this striped pattern, which was designed in Illustrator, across the body of the tube. It will give your 3D model more character and help visually align it with other products that are part of this campaign.

The exercise files for this chapter also include a file named *label.png*. This file is a label designed in Adobe Express specifically for the product itself, which is a skin cream that wards off bothersome mosquitoes in the warmer months.

With both branding images in mind (and on-hand), you'll now apply them to the cream tube 3D model.

Working with the Background Pattern

You will place the background pattern on the tube first and then place the label. Of course, you can always adjust the stacking order of these images afterward, but it is better to start in the proper placement order.

1. Return to the Substance 3D Stager *mosquito.ssg* project and select the **body_mesh** object in the **cream_tube** group from the **Scene** panel.

   You will be applying image assets only to this mesh.

2. In the **Properties** panel, select the **Material** tab. The **Shinny Plastic** material should be selected, as it is the only material available.

3. Click the **Place Image On Model** button  below the Shinny Plastic material.

    A file browser dialog box appears.

4. Select the file *pattern.png* and click **Open**.

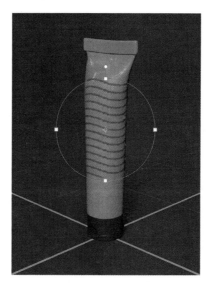

The image is mapped roughly onto the surface of the tube.

5. In the **Properties** panel, ensure the **Graphic** material is selected and change the **Placement** setting from Decal to **Fill**.

    Decal placement treats the image asset like a sticker or label, while Fill placement stretches the image out across the entire mesh to fill every last bit.

6. Ensure you have the **Select** tool chosen. A transform overlay will appear across the image applied to the object.

7. Adjust the following values of the image until you get an interesting result:

- **Position:** Drag the image in the transform overlay.

- **Rotation:** Drag the little circle that protrudes from the overlay.

- **Repeat:** Drag the four squares around the overlay.

  These properties can also be adjusted through the **Offset** and **Repeat** properties in the **Properties** panel when an image is selected in the Material tab.

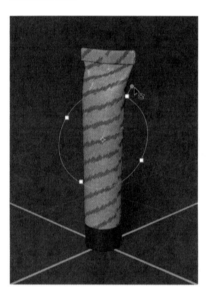

I used the settings shown in the image for my example.

Working with the Label

To complete the tube design, you will place the label image on the tube, overlaying both the material and the pattern image.

1. Select the **Shinny Plastic** material in the **Material** section of the **Properties** panel.

2. Click the **Place Image On Model** button ⬛ beneath the material.

   If a graphic is selected instead of the underlying material, the Place Image On Model button ⬛ will not appear.

3. In the file browser dialog box that appears, select the image file *label.png* and click **Open**.

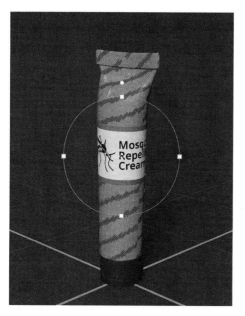

NOTE You might have worried that because you selected the material, which is visually placed beneath the pattern image in the Properties panel, the new image would appear beneath the pattern image. This would be the case in other software, like Adobe Photoshop, but in Substance 3D Stager, these image layers are always added to the top of the stack no matter what.

The label image is placed on the tube as a decal, and a transform overlay appears around it.

4. Use the transform overlay to adjust the **Position**, **Rotation**, and **Scale** properties of the label so that it sits squarely on the front surface of the tube.

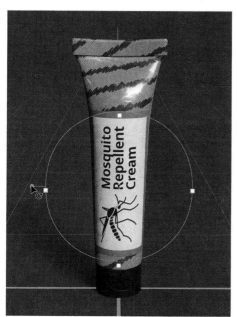

NOTE You can adjust the stacking order of images placed on a model. To do so, simply drag each image to a new position in the Material tab of the Properties panel. You cannot move a material up and down the stack—only images. To layer materials, you can use other tools, like Substance 3D Painter, as you did in Chapter 6.

5. Adjust the camera view if necessary to change your view and achieve the ideal placement for the label. Chapter 6 covered how this can be done with the Orbit ⟳, Pan ✛, and Dolly ⬇ tools.

    The 3D model design is now complete!

6. Switch the **Ray Tracing** toggle [Ray tracing] to the active position to view the cream tube in a more realistic way.

    This renders a more realistic preview of the product, with all materials and images applied.

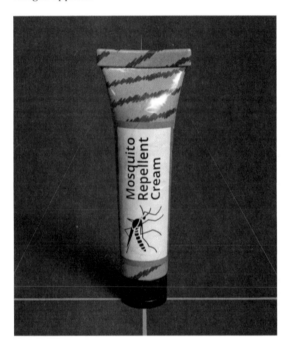

    Notice that the label and pattern images conform to the creases and deviations across the tube because they were placed on the Shinny Plastic material. And Ray Tracing renders reflections and shadows in a much more complex and realistic manner.

7. Once you are finished admiring your work, switch the **Ray Tracing** toggle [Ray tracing] to the inactive position.

    Ray Tracing takes much more computing power to render your content than the real-time preview render, so it should be used sparingly.

Exporting 3D Models for After Effects

You are nearly finished with Substance 3D Stager and will soon move to After Effects to design motion content using your newly designed 3D model. The only thing left to do is export the design in a format that is compatible with the Advanced 3D render engine.

1. Choose **File** > **Export** > **Scene** from the application menu.

   The **Export Scene** dialog box appears with the default settings.

   After Effects supports only the 3D model formats GLB and GLTF in the Advanced 3D render engine. I suggest exporting as GLB, as this produces a single file instead of a collection of files (as GLTF would).

2. Select **GLB** from the **Format** drop-down.

   The other settings in the dialog box work fine for our purposes, but if you need to, you can change the **Save To** location to something more accessible to you.

3. Click **Export** to complete the export process.

   The export is saved as a GLB file in the location you specified.

   If you ever choose to create a GLTF file, you will have a set of files to deal with instead of just one.

Creating Simple 3D Motion in Substance 3D Stager

Before jumping back into After Effects, note that Substance 3D Stager also features a set of motion design tools, however simplistic.

To access a timeline that appears along the bottom of the interface, click the **Timeline** button  in the lower left of the interface. Once animation is added to an object in your project, you can control the playback through the timeline controls.

To add animation to an object, access the **Properties** panel with that object selected and then click the **Animation** tab to reveal the set of animation choices.

Substance 3D Stager includes two animation choices that are activated with a toggle switch: Orbit and Spin.

- **Orbit:** Activates animation that enables one object to orbit another. This is very useful when applied to a camera or a light. You must also specify the target object it will orbit around.

- **Spin:** A bit simpler than Orbit, this choice activates animation that spins the selected object around. This is best to use when you want to showcase all sides of an object.

The animation choices share several properties:

- **Target Offset:** This offsets your motion by a distance measured in centimeters along each of the three axes. The default is no offset at all, with each being a value of 0 cm.

- **Duration:** This determines how long or short your animation is. The default is 3 seconds.

- **Rotation:** Measured in degrees, this determines how much of a full 360° rotation is achieved across the given duration. The default is, of course, the full 360°.

- **Reverse:** This checkbox reverses the direction of your motion when activated.

- **Easing:** This set of common easing algorithms adds a bit of weight and dynamic physicality to the motion.

Of course, you want to have full control over any motion given to your 3D model, and that is where After Effects steps in.

3D Motion Design in After Effects

Now that you have a well-designed 3D model, you can begin creating an After Effects composition that uses the Advanced 3D rendering engine. You'll start by creating a new project, importing your GLB file, and animating it across a 3D composition.

Creating a New Composition

Before you can use the 3D model you've designed in Substance 3D Stager, you'll need to create a new After Effects composition and save your project.

1. In After Effects, click the **New Project** button on the Home screen or choose **New** > **New Project** from the application menu.

    The Home screen disappears, and you are prompted to create a new composition.

2. Click the large **New Composition** button in the center of the screen, or choose **Composition** > **New Composition** from the application menu, to create a new composition.

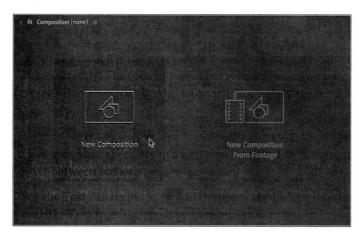

    The Composition Settings dialog box appears.

3. In the **Composition Settings** dialog box, enter **Mosquito** for the **Composition Name** and choose **Social Media Landscape – 1280x720 – 30 fps** from the **Preset** menu. Set **Duration** to **0:00:10:00** (10 seconds) and choose black (**#000000**) for the **Background Color**.

TIP Remember early in this chapter when we looked at the 3D Renderer tab and the options in it? You could adjust the 3D renderer at this point, but you don't need to because the act of adding a 3D model to a composition automatically triggers the switch to Advanced 3D.

4. Click **OK**.

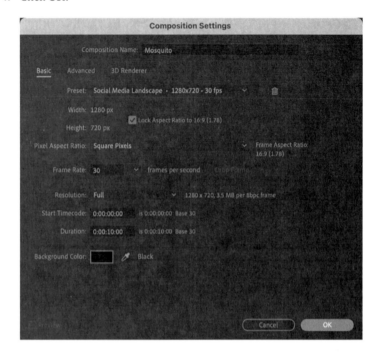

The **Composition Settings** dialog box closes, and a new composition is created according to your choices.

5. Save your project by choosing **File** > **Save** from the application menu.

   A save dialog box appears.

6. Choose a location for the file on your computer and name the file *Mosquito.aep*.

7. Click **Save**.

You now have a new After Effects project file that contains a single empty composition. You will spend the remainder of this chapter working in the composition just created.

Importing a 3D Model

You spent a lot of time in Substance 3D Stager designing the cream tube model, layering it with branding assets, and tweaking everything so it appears just as you like. You'll now import that model into After Effects to use it in your composition.

3D model files are imported into After Affects much like any other asset.

1. Ensure your **Project** panel is open and locate the file *mosquito.glb*, which you exported from Substance 3D Stager.

   The only item in your **Project** panel is your **Mosquito** composition.

2. Drag *mosquito.glb* directly onto the **Project** panel from your file system to add it to the panel. It will appear as a folder named Mosquito.

3. Open the Mosquito folder to reveal the *mosquito.glb* file inside it.

NOTE You could also choose File > Import > File from the application menu to locate and import your 3D model. Either method provides the same result.

Recall that a GLB file contains all meshes, textures, and other assets in a single file. If you were to import a GLTF file, you would see many different types of assets in this folder—perhaps even subfolders.

The Mosquito composition should be open in the timeline below. If it is not, double-click it in the Project panel to open it in the timeline.

You will need the composition open to add the 3D model to it.

4. Add the *mosquito.glb* file to the Mosquito composition by dragging it from the **Project** panel into the timeline.

Drop the file into the left or right area of the timeline; it makes no difference.

The **Model Settings** dialog box appears, and you can make adjustments to how your model appears in the composition.

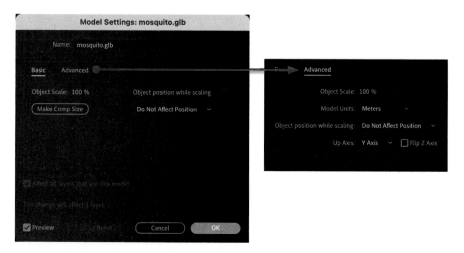

This dialog box offers choices for how your 3D model will scale in the composition and how its position is affected when scaling. The **Basic** tab focuses on object scaling, and the **Advanced** tab allows you to choose the units used to measure the scale and which of the three axes determines what is considered "up" for this model, determining how the gizmo overlay appears and how each axis influences the model.

NOTE Now that a 3D model has been added to the composition, Advanced 3D appears as the selected renderer in the lower right of the Composition panel.

5. Select **Do Not Affect Position** from the **Object Position While Scaling** drop-down if it is not already selected. Leave Object Scale and the other parameters at their default values, and click **OK**.

Now that the 3D model is available in the composition, you can see it is quite small and not ideally positioned to fill the frame.

6. To adjust its appearance, choose the **Selection** tool  from the tools at the top of the interface. Ensure that the *mosquito.glb* layer is selected, and use the gizmo overlay to adjust the scale, rotation, and position of your 3D model to view the details of your work so far.

In the figure, I've adjusted my object so that it better fills the frame, and the details of the materials, patterned background, and label can be easily viewed and appreciated.

Don't worry about getting the tube positioned and scaled in any meaningful way just yet; you'll be more precise in the next section, when you begin animating the object across time.

Adding Motion to the 3D Model

Now that the 3D model is imported and included in a composition, it's time to add some motion to it! Although this is a new capability of After Effects, the process for giving motion to a 3D model is conveniently the same as with just about any other asset.

1. Open the **Transform** properties of the *mosquito.glb* layer and move the playhead to the 4-second position, **0:00:04:00**.

2. Click each **Stopwatch** toggle 🔘 to the left of the **Position**, **Scale**, and **Orientation** properties.

Keyframes are inserted at the 4 second mark along the timeline for the chosen transform properties.

The most direct way to set up your motion design is to start with the end.

3. Use the gizmo overlay or adjust the numeric transform properties to place the tube product in a prominent position in the composition frame.

If you would prefer direct values for these properties, set them as follows:

- Position: **190, 465, -55**

- Scale: **1080%, 1080%, 1080%**

- Orientation: **0°, 7°, 80°**

This results in a tube that fills the screen while facing the viewer and being slightly tilted to keep the view interesting.

You can always deviate from these choices if desired, of course. Just remember that if you do so your results may differ from the figures in this chapter.

Now, let's set the second set of keyframes.

4. Move your playhead to the 2-second mark along the timeline, **0:00:02:00**, and click the **Insert Keyframe** icon to the left of the property name to duplicate keyframes for the **Position**, **Scale**, and **Orientation** properties.

This sets these property values to be identical across time between the two sets of keyframes you created.

You should have identical keyframes for **Position**, **Scale**, and **Orientation** properties at both 0:00:02:00 and 0:00:04:00 along the timeline.

The tube of cream should emerge from the bottom of the screen to the previously set **Position**, **Scale**, and **Orientation** property settings.

You should be at the first keyframe, at 0:00:02:00, which is your starting point.

Next, you will set the 3D model so that it is much smaller in scale, rotated differently from its final value, and positioned out of frame beyond the bottom of the composition.

5. Using either the gizmo overlay or the numeric property values to adjust the following transform properties:

- Position: **250, 1200, 1640**

- Scale: **345%, 345%, 345%**

- Orientation: **295°, 325°, 30°**

Again, you may deviate from these values, but the result will differ from what you see here.

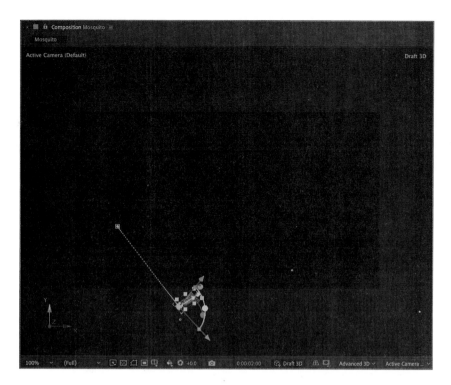

The tube should be rather small and appear lost in blackness at this point. You will, of course, embellish the composition with additional artifacts to keep things interesting for the viewer, but the motion of the centerpiece tube asset is of primary importance.

TIP Chapter 5 explained that you can enable Draft 3D mode to view content outside the frame in your composition. This is useful when you want an object to emerge from outside the frame and into full view.

If you play back the motion you've created, it will be very linear and not so interesting. You can fix this by applying easing to the keyframes.

6. Using the **Selection** tool , drag a selection rectangle across all the keyframes in the timeline.

The selected keyframes are highlighted in blue.

7. Choose **Animation** > **Keyframe Assistant** > **Easy Ease** from the application menu to create simple easing across the selected keyframes.

The selected keyframes change from a diamond shape to an hourglass, indicating that an ease has been applied.

This action produces a much more dynamic and physical motion across the keyframes' property transitions. Play back your composition to see how much smoother the animation is now.

The tube emerges from the bottom of the screen, rotates slightly, scales up, and settles into position in the center of the frame. The primary motion for this composition is now complete.

Compositing with Additional Elements

At this point in the project, you've imported and granted dynamic motion to the 3D model of the mosquito repellent cream product. Yet, it exists in a black void and could be more engaging for the viewer. You will now add some additional design elements, including an AI-generated background, some 3D text, and environmental lighting derived from HDRi panoramic imagery.

Generating Background Content with Adobe Firefly

Although you could use stock photography or commission artwork or a photograph as a background for your motion design, you have options for creating all sorts of assets through generative AI platforms.

Adobe Firefly is a new set of generative AI tools that you can access via *https://firefly.adobe.com/*. It is increasingly being integrated into traditional products like Photoshop, Illustrator, and Express.

Firefly has many advantages over its competitors. It has been ethically trained on a dataset of Adobe Stock materials along with openly licensed work and public domain content with expired copyright. Other generative AI services have been trained on content simply scraped from the open web, which is problematic because copyrighted materials are included in such a dataset. When using Firefly, this is not a concern.

Additionally, Adobe has declared that content generated through Firefly is commercially viable. You do not have to worry about whether someone is going to come after you and declare that you've stolen their work.

Let's use Firefly to create a suitable background for your motion content.

1. In your web browser, visit *https://firefly.adobe.com/* and locate one of the **Text To Image** modules that are prominently displayed on the page.

2. In the text prompt field, enter **soft texture consisting of greens and oranges, very dark, painterly strokes, obscured by mist** and click the **Generate** button to have Firefly interpret your text prompt into a visual asset.

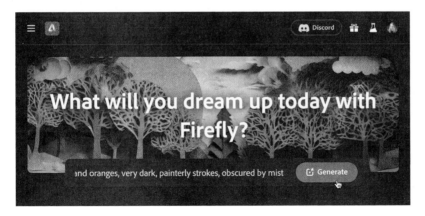

Being as descriptive as possible with your text prompt is likely to achieve results that more closely match what you envision.

The results appear, along with several additional options in the right column that you can tweak to improve or modify the visuals generated through the initial prompt. Since your After Effects composition is framed at a 16:9 resolution, you should tweak the Aspect Ratio value.

3. Select **Widescreen (16:9)** in the **Aspect Ratio** drop-down.

I also selected **Photo** for the **Content Type** and used **Firefly Image 2** for the generative AI model.

Below these choices are even more ways of tweaking the resulting imagery.

4. Select the following values to tweak the result:

- Color and Tone: **Warm Tone**

- Lighting: **Dramatic Light**

- Composition: **Wide Angle**

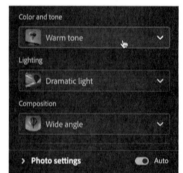

These options generate a visual of a hot, muggy environment that's prone to be inhabited by many mosquitoes.

The **Prompt** area below the images reflects the choices made by adding tags alongside the original text prompt.

You can remove these tags, if desired, by clicking the small x icon to the right of each tag.

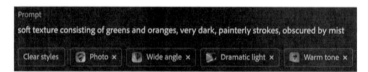

You can also adjust the initial text prompt from here to further refine the results being generated.

5. Click **Refresh**  to the right of the text prompt to refresh the generated visuals based on your refinements.

A new set of four images is generated.

6. Click the image that most closely matches your vision to view it in greater detail.

7. Select the **More Options** icon in the upper right of the image to download the image to your computer for use in After Effects and other applications.

TIP When using After Effects, it is always best to keep all your source assets in the same folder so as not to mistakenly delete or lose anything that is necessary to the project.

The image asset downloads to your computer as a high-resolution JPEG.

The image I produced measures 2688 pixels wide and 1536 pixels high. This is much larger than the After Effects composition that it was created for and should work well as a background element for the motion design.

Now that you have a suitable background image—thanks to Firefly—you can complete the After Effects composition.

Adding the Generated Background Image

Now that you have a suitable background asset, it is time to compose it in the motion design.

It will not be animated, but subtle panning or scaling might be appropriate, if desired.

1. Drag the Firefly-generated JPEG from your system file browser into the **Project** panel, or choose **File** > **Import** > **File** from the application menu, to import it.

The imported image appears in the **Project** panel.

2. Drag the imported image into the **Timeline** panel to add it as a layer. Be sure to drag it to the lowest point in the layer stack so that it appears behind the tube.

Since the resolution of the image from Firefly is greater than that of your composition, you'll need to make it a 3D-enabled layer and make some other adjustments.

3. Click the **3D Layer** toggle ⬡ to the right of the layer name, and set the following property values in the **Properties** panel or via the layer transform properties group in the timeline:

   - Scale: **85%**

   - Position: **640, 360, 1335** in.

   This ensures the background image is placed behind the tube in 3D space and that it is scaled appropriately.

NOTE You need to activate the stopwatch only when working with a change in property values over time through keyframes. Simply adjusting properties without the stopwatch active, as you've done here, adjusts the object's properties across the entire span of the timeline without motion.

The background image generated with Firefly integrates perfectly with the tube model from Substance 3D Stager. You really do get the feel of an oppressive, humid, mosquito-filled environment with this combination of assets!

You aren't finished with this composition yet, though; you still need to add text content and adjust the lighting.

Firefly and 3D Workflows

Although you used Firefly in this project to generate background imagery, there are many more possible workflows with generative AI and 3D-capable software applications as part of Adobe Creative Cloud and Substance 3D.

A great example of this is material generation in Substance 3D Sampler. You saw how to generate your own materials using this software in Chapter 2. Of course, you can also generate very realistic materials using content generated with Firefly and then transformed in Substance 3D Sampler.

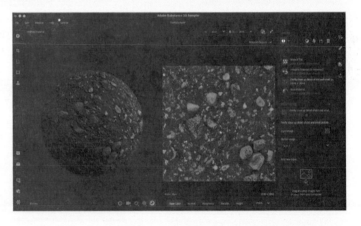

The prompt used to create these textures, for example, was "closeup detail of dirt and small pebbles from above." As with all things generative AI, the more specific your prompt is, the more likely the resulting image will conform to your request.

Also of note are more direct 3D integrations through Firefly, as showcased through beta experiments such as Project Gingerbread, a service that leverages Firefly capabilities to generate visuals through a combination of 3D primitives and generative text prompts. These elements work together to influence the composition and structure of the resulting visual that is generated. This is a great example of what to expect from generative AI in the months and years ahead.

Creating 3D Text

You are approaching the completion of this project. The addition of a suitable background image has certainly helped create a fully formed composition in After Effects, but there is more to be done.

You will now add text that implores the viewer to purchase the product before summer strikes and the mosquitoes are out in full force.

1. Choose the **Text** tool from the tools at the top of the interface, and click in the top left of the **Composition** panel to create a new text object.

2. Type **Buy Before Summer!** for the text content.

3. In the **Properties** panel, set the following values:

   - Position: **55** for x and **125** for y

   - Typeface: **Arial Black**

   - Text size: **72px**

   - Text fill color: **#FFE972** (light yellow)

   - Use the alignment options in the paragraph properties to **left-align** the text.

The text appears across the background image. Since similar colors are present in the image and the text, some of the text is difficult to read.

NOTE If you do not have Arial Black available, substitute a typeface that is similar in weight and appearance, although you may need to adjust other properties if you do so.

You can remedy this in several ways, but here you will use the Advanced 3D renderer to transform your text to native 3D.

4. In the timeline, click the **Enable 3D Layer** toggle ⬡ for the newly created text layer.

   The text object now includes additional 3D properties, thanks to the Advanced 3D renderer.

5. To provide a more 3D appearance to the text, open the layer properties and then the **Geometry Options** and **Material Options** property groups.

   These property groups are available because the text is a 3D layer. Additional properties are available in the **Transform** property group, similar to what you saw in Chapter 5.

6. Change **Bevel Style** to **Angular** and adjust the **Extrusion Depth** value to **10**.

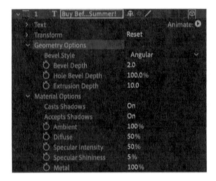

With these changes made to the text properties, a visible bevel surrounds the edges of each character, greatly improving readability.

With the text element created and transformed to a 3D object, the only thing left to do with this object is transition it into view through a small bit of animation.

Animating 3D Text

The text message should appear only after the animation of the 3D tube has completed. Right now, the text is always present across the entire composition. You will now prepare the text for animation and use standard keyframing techniques to perform a small transition.

1. Using the **Selection** tool ![cursor], right-click the text in the **Composition** panel, and align the anchor point to the visual center of the text by choosing **Transform > Center Anchor Point in Layer Content** from the context menu.

This causes properties such as **Scale** and **Rotate** to align to the center of the text instead of to the left edge, which was the original placement of the anchor point.

2. Move the playhead to the 5-second mark, at **0:00:05:00**, and open the **Transform** properties group.

3. Enable the **Stopwatch** toggle ![stopwatch] for the **Scale** and **Opacity** properties.

   You will use these properties to design a short fade-in transition where the text scales up a small amount.

4. Move the playhead a bit to the right, to **0:00:05:13**, and click the **Insert Keyframe** button ![diamond] to the left of the Scale and Opacity properties.

   This duplicates the previous keyframes for both properties, which ensures these properties retain their current values at the end of the transition.

5. Leave the keyframe values at 0:00:05:13 at 100% and click the **Go to Previous Keyframe** button ![previous] to the left of either property to return to the keyframes at 0:00:05:00.

6. Adjust **Scale** to **66%** and **Opacity** to **0%**.

These changes make the text initially transparent and 66% smaller.

Now let's finish the motion off with a bit of easing.

7. Select all four keyframes by dragging a selection rectangle around them in the timeline.

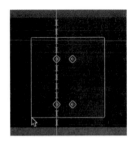

The keyframes are highlighted with a blue outline.

8. Choose **Animation** > **Keyframe Assistant** > **Easy Ease** from the application menu.

The diamond-shaped keyframes transform into small hourglass shapes, indicating that an ease has been applied.

9. Play back the full composition to view the results of your work.

All the animation is now complete, but there are still a few items left to examine before you close out this project.

Applying an HDRi Image as an Environmental Light

The Advanced 3D rendering engine allows for a new type of lighting, based on HDRi photography.

Included in the files for this chapter is an image named *rainforest_trail_8k.hdr.*

Image sourced from https://hdri-haven.com/hdri/tropical-forest

This is an HDRi file that has been downloaded from HDRI-HAVEN, although you can use any HDRi photo that you like, of course. The image file is a high-resolution, equirectangular 360° photo taken in a rainforest environment. This is perfect for your mosquito composition.

You will now create a new environment light and use the HDRi image for its source. You will first get the HDRi file into the existing composition so that you can use it.

1. Choose **File** > **Import** > **File** from the application menu and select the .*hdr* file. Alternatively, drag the file into the Project panel from your system file browser.

2. Click **Open**.

3. Drag the .*hdr* file from the **Project** panel to the bottom of the layer stack in the timeline.

Since the image is going to be used as a source for the light you will create, it doesn't need to be visible to the viewer in any way. Placing it at the very bottom of the layer stack completely obscures it from view.

4. Select the top layer in the composition layer stack—this should be the text layer—and then choose **Layer** > **New** > **Light** from the application menu.

   The **Light Settings** dialog box appears, allowing you to make choices about what sort of light to create and its specific properties.

5. In the **Light Settings** dialog box, choose **Environment** from the **Light Type** menu and click **OK**.

   A new light named Environment Light 1 is created and added as a new layer at the top of the layer stack.

6. Open the layer properties and then the **Light Options** group.

7. Click the **Source** dropdown and select the HDRi image layer.

Because After Effects is aware that this layer contains HDRi data, it is presented as a source option for use in this light. Non-HDRi images will not appear in this drop-down.

The composition takes on a look that is much more overcast—as though beneath a vast jungle environment and potentially filled with mosquitoes.

Although the environment light has the intended effect on the look of the composition, you can add additional light to bring focus directly onto the centerpiece.

8. Select the topmost layer in the layer stack and choose **Layer** > **New** > **Light** from the application menu.

   The **Light Settings** dialog box appears.

9. In the **Light Settings** dialog box, choose **Point** for the **Light Type** and enter **#F45922** (bright orange) for the **Color**.

10. Click **OK**.

   A new point light is added to the composition, making the lighting more intense across the cream tube.

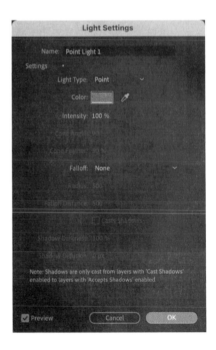

If desired, you can adjust the position of the point light and other properties to achieve the exact look you want.

With the lighting taken care of, your 3D-motion design is complete.

Rendering the 3D Motion Design

Now that you've completed the composition, it's time to render it for distribution. When you created the composition, the duration was set to 10 seconds. Although this provides a good amount of wiggle room for designing motion, 10 seconds is a bit too lengthy for the final output. That's okay because After Effects includes mechanisms that allow you to render a specific segment of the composition.

You'll now set the work area to render and produce a distributable MP4 video file. By default, the work area is set to the entire duration of the composition. To set it to include a segment of the composition, you'll adjust the work area start and only end markers at the top of the timeline—located above the layers but below the time marks.

TIP You can also use keyboard shortcuts to set the marker definitions. Move the playhead to 01s and press B to set the Work Area Start marker; then move the playhead to 08s and press N to set the Work Area End marker. This is especially useful if you are not sure which markers to adjust, since there are a few along the timeline.

1. Locate the **Work Area Start** marker, at 0:00:00:00, and drag it to the **01s** mark. Similarly, locate the **Work Area End** marker, at 0:00:10:00, and drag it to the **08s** mark.

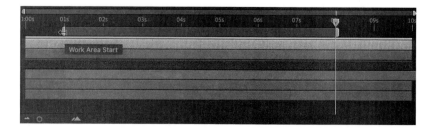

This effectively trims the resulting content. When rendering this composition, only the work area you've defined will be rendered into the final MP4 video.

2. Be sure that the composition is selected in either the **Project** panel or the timeline, and choose **Composition** > **Add to Render Queue** from the application menu.

    The render queue opens alongside the composition timeline, and a new job displays.

3. Ensure that **Output Module** is set to **H.264 – Match Render Settings – 15 Mbps** and set the **Output To** name and location.

4. Click the **Render** button.

The composition work area is rendered as an MP4 video file to the location and name you specified.

5. Locate the file on your computer.

    The duration should be 7 seconds, since that is how you defined the work area in the composition timeline.

That's it! You've completed the project. You've used many skills and workflows to produce this 3D motion design across Adobe Express, Illustrator, Substance 3D Stager, Firefly, and After Effects. It is truly amazing what can be achieved through the combination of 2D and 3D software.

In the next chapter, we'll consider several additional workflows and related techniques.

CHAPTER 10

Where to Go Next

In this final chapter, we'll cover a variety of additional software applications within Adobe Substance 3D and Adobe Creative Cloud collections, some that we've partially explored and others that are entirely new. This chapter provides an overview of additional 3D design elements and virtual reality (VR) tools you can explore once you are finished with this book.

We'll examine how to contribute your creations to the Substance 3D Community Assets library, introduce additional software applications that are part of Adobe Substance 3D—Modeler and Designer—and then investigate 3D and VR workflows in Creative Cloud applications that use newer features in Adobe Photoshop and Adobe Illustrator. We conclude by exploring additional virtual reality possibilities in Adobe Animate and Adobe Premiere Pro.

Contributing Content to the Substance 3D Community Assets Library

Chapter 1 introduced the Substance 3D Assets and Substance 3D Community Assets libraries. It explored these libraries and explained how to download models and materials for use in 3D design projects.

You—as a 3D designer—can act as a contributor to the Substance 3D Community Assets library. If you have created materials or models you'd like to share, clicking the Upload button once authenticated into the library will allow you to do so.

Here is how the process works.

1. Ensure you are logged in with your Adobe ID to *https://substance3d.adobe.com/community-assets*.

2. Click the **Upload** button in the upper right of your browser viewport.

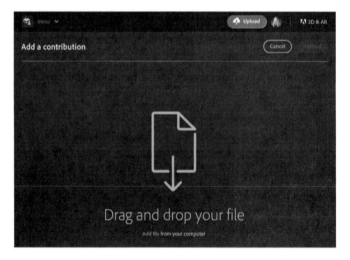

A screen appears, prompting you to choose a file to submit.

3. Locate the file on your hard drive that you want to submit and drag it onto the **Drag and Drop Your File** prompt.

The chosen file is uploaded, and the screen switches to the file contribution view.

4. Under **File Type**, choose the type of asset you are submitting.

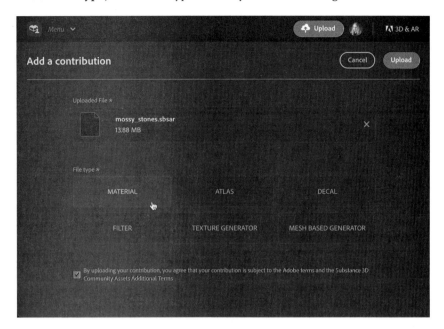

You will be prompted to agree to the community terms.

5. Activate the checkbox below the **File Type** selection area to agree to the community terms.

6. Click the **Upload** button that appears once you have identified the file type and agreed to the terms.

The publish screen displays for you to make final adjustments to the submission.

7. Modify the title and description of your asset submission, identify which categories it should be organized within, tag it with a set of keywords, and then click the **Publish** button.

Your submission is now part of the Substance 3D Community Assets library!

The asset appears alongside contributions from your fellow community members. Using the categories, keywords, title, and description that you assigned upon submission should help you—and others—easily locate the asset.

Anything new appears on the front page of the website, and following a successful submission, users can immediately locate your asset.

8. Click your submitted asset to display a details page that allows you, as the contributor, to make changes by clicking the **Update** button.

This asset details page allows users to view asset details, see what software applications are compatible with the chosen asset, and download your submission for use in their own 3D design projects.

Exploring Additional 3D Design Workflows

You can work with 3D design assets in many ways across both Substance 3D and Creative Cloud. The previous chapters explored many of these capabilities, but with all things creative, there is more to explore! With the foundation you now have in using these applications to design projects across a variety of media, you may consider exploring these additional software applications and 3D design workflows.

Sculpting with Substance 3D Modeler

Substance 3D Modeler is the newest addition to Substance 3D and is perhaps the most ambitious element of the entire collection. While traditional 3D-modeling software takes a very precise and programmatic approach to the creation of 3D models, Substance 3D Modeler approaches 3D modeling from the perspective of a sculptor working with clay.

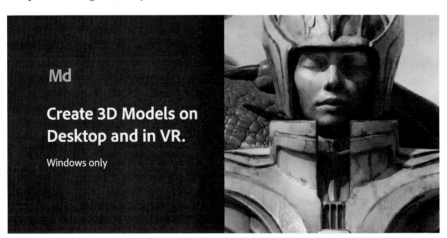

Substance 3D Modeler boasts the following features:

- **Desktop and virtual reality support:** Switch seamlessly between modes to adapt your preferences or to meet the needs of a specific 3D-modeling project.

- **Symmetry and repetition tools:** Work efficiently and accurately with these built-in tools to assemble complex objects or craft with incredible detail.

- **Organic sculpting:** Build, smooth, and shape organically with digital 3D-sculpting tools inspired by real-world clay.

NOTE If you are on macOS—or just want a more traditional modeling experience— Blender is also a great choice (*www.blender .org*).

- **Hard surface sculpting:** Create clear, decisive forms using parametric shapes. Easily add and cut primitives to form complex models.

Although Substance 3D Modeler is a Windows-only product for now, macOS support is said to be coming.

Procedural Material Creation with Substance 3D Designer

One of the more intimidating applications in the Substance 3D software is Substance 3D Designer. It features a node-based, procedural design system that is foreign to most traditional 2D workflows. Using Substance 3D Designer, you can generate infinite texture variations from procedural patterns inside these complex node-based graphs.

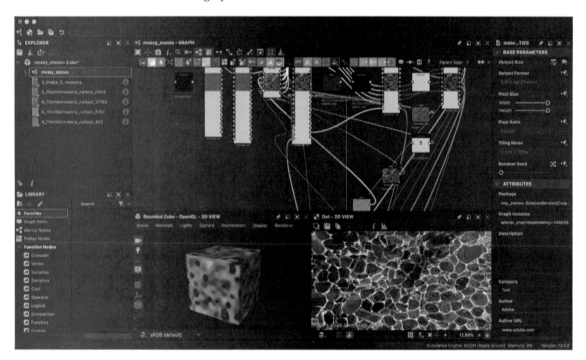

Substance 3D Designer boasts the following features:

- **Ever-growing content library:** Access hundreds of nodes, filters, patterns, and randomizable noises.

- **HDR lighting creation:** Build parametric lighting stages using procedural lights or 360° images.

- **Color management:** Take advantage of Pantone and OpenColorIO support. OpenColorIO is a color management solution used in film, visual effects, and motion design.

- **MDL support:** Create material definition language (MDL) materials with the dedicated shader graph. Using MDL allows a designer to create materials that can simulate the behavior of real-world textures and objects in a virtual environment.

- **Open ecosystem:** Easily send your materials and filters to other Substance 3D apps.

Although this application takes a different approach to material generation than something like Substance 3D Sampler, it is a powerful way of designing complex and realistic materials for film, gaming, television, and more.

Parametric Filters in Adobe Photoshop (beta)

Parametric filters are the primary tool used to modify and adjust assets across several Substance 3D applications—including Substance 3D Sampler. As you continue to see workflow and feature crossovers between Adobe Creative Cloud and Adobe Substance 3D software, parametric filters are becoming an integrated part of traditional 2D workflows.

TIP You can use the export functionality of Substance 3D Sampler to edit a material designed in that application within Substance 3D Designer—giving you a head start on the complicated node structure it uses. Just choose Export > Send to Substance 3D Designer.

NOTE Custom parametric filters are normally created with Substance 3D Designer. After designing your filter, it must be exported as a Substance Archive file (*.sbsar*) for use in other software, such as Photoshop.

You have encountered parametric filters before in this book—during the previous exploration of Substance 3D Sampler. In that application, filters are applied in a layer stack to influence the photographic content you began the project with. In Photoshop, you now have access to similar parametric filters—although since this is Photoshop, they are applied to layers as filters, conforming to traditional Photoshop design workflows.

NOTE For this exercise you'll be using a Photoshop file named *parametric.psd* that is included in the exercise files for this chapter.

To apply a parametric filter to your content, you select the layer that contains the artwork you want to be affected and choose the filter you'd like to use from the **Parametric Filters** panel. You'll access this panel in this exercise to apply a filter to a layer. The layer contains a logo that has been imported into the Photoshop document to give it the appearance of a vinyl sticker.

1. In the **Layers** panel, right-click the *logo* layer thumbnail in the *parametric.psd* file.

   A context menu appears.

2. Choose the **Select Pixels** option.

A marching ants–style selection displays around the logo.

Next, you will choose the parametric filter you want to apply.

3. Choose **Filter** > **Parametric Filters** from the application menu.

The **Parametric Filters** panel appears.

The panel displays several parametric filters that you can immediately use in your Photoshop compositions. These filters are applied individually to selected layers.

Parametric filters range from common adjustments such as applying a duotone effect to an image to more physical filters such as applying the look of a vinyl sticker to the selected content.

NOTE Upon first use of parametric filters in a composition, Photoshop downloads the default set of filters to your computer.

4. In the **Parametric Filters** panel, select the filter named *Sticker Filter*.

    The chosen parametric filter is applied to the selected layer as a Smart Filter. Because you made a selection in the selected layer, a layer mask is also created, confining the filter effect to the selection.

TIP You can use selections and other masking techniques in Photoshop to automatically mask the application of any chosen parametric filter.

Once the filter is applied, another panel appears that can be used to tweak the various properties of your filter. This is the **Parametric Properties** panel and is specific to the properties associated with this type of filter.

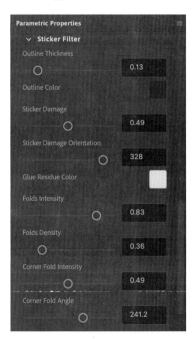

TIP You can always access the Parametric Properties panel by double-clicking the parametric filter itself in the Layers panel. This is good to know in case you close the panel and then later need to work in it again.

Your chosen filter will likely include many properties that can be adjusted. Be sure to scroll down to view all the properties specific to each parametric filter. You can adjust these properties through the available sliders, drop-downs, color chips, and numeric inputs.

Adjusting the specific properties of these filters enables you to dial in the specific look you desire and make the original asset appear quite different.

Unmodified logo   Parametric filter applied

With the filter applied and properties like **Sticker Damage** and **Folds Intensity** bumped up, the appearance of the logo is drastically altered, and it appears very much like a damaged vinyl sticker.

5. Click the small plus button ✚ at the bottom of the **Parametric Filters** panel to add your own parametric filters and Substance 3D materials to this panel.

They will appear under **Your Filters**.

Once you've added your own filters to the **Parametric Filters** panel, you can apply them to layers and adjust them just like the standard set of filters.

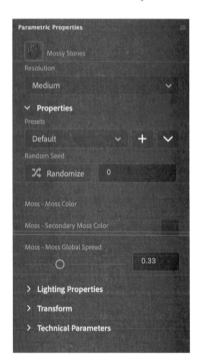

Materials created in Substance 3D Sampler or Substance 3D Designer will even expose the designer-specified properties, just as in other applications. Taking the Mossy Stones material as an example, you can adjust **Moss Color**, **Secondary Moss Color**, and **Moss Global Spread** from this panel, since you marked those properties to be adjustable when the material was designed.

Of course, you can combine parametric filters on different layers in your composition—very similarly to how you used the **Materials** panel in Chapter 3. In the next figure, I've applied the Sticker Filter to the logo, but I've also used the Mossy Stones material generated using Substance 3D Sampler in Chapter 2.

These intersections between parametric filters, materials, and more in Substance 3D are expected to continue to grow as the software evolves.

Mockup in Adobe Illustrator (beta)

Although not strictly a 3D feature in Illustrator, Mockup does provide the appearance of 3D to vector graphics by analyzing a photograph using artificial intelligence and creating an underlying depth mesh that can be used to apply the selected vector graphic along curved surfaces. This is an incredibly useful feature when mocking up your designs on real-world objects.

You'll use the same logo as you did in the previous section along with a photograph of a curved piece of building material. The logo is a vector group, and the photograph is a bitmap image.

NOTE In this exercise you'll be using an Illustrator file named *mockup.ai* that is included in the exercise files for this chapter.

The vector logo and photographic bitmap image exist on the artboard in a single Illustrator layer.

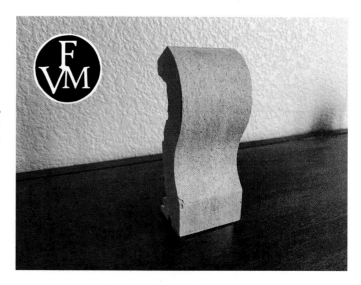

1. Open *mockup.ai* from the exercise files in Illustrator.

2. To use the Mockup feature, ensure that the vector object and photograph you want to use are both selected.

3. With both pieces of content selected, choose **Object** > **Mockup** > **Make** from the application menu.

The Mockup feature uses artificial intelligence to determine the form of all visual objects present in the photograph.

The vector artwork is transformed into a symbol, and both it and the photograph are placed in a new Mockup object. The Mockup object is a special object type in Illustrator.

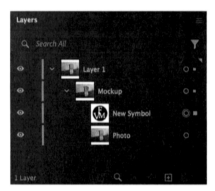

With a Mockup object successfully created, you can select the logo vector artwork symbol and move it across the various visual objects represented by the underlying photograph.

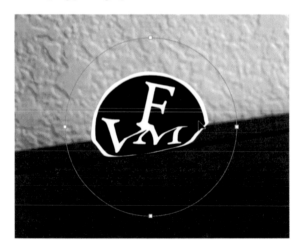

Because of the underlying mesh created by the AI, which is based on the perceived depth and form properties of the photograph and the objects in it, the logo automatically conforms to and wraps around the perceived objects in the photograph.

For instance, moving the logo across the artboard and over the curved surface of the stone tile results in the symbol visually adhering to the form of the stone.

TIP The symbol can be scaled up or down in size by using the Mockup control handles that appear when the object is selected.

You can always edit the mockup.

4. Select the symbol within it or select the Mockup object and choose **Object** > **Mockup** > **Edit** from the application menu.

An additional feature of the Mockup workflow is in the **Mockup** panel.

5. Choose **Window** > **Mockup** from the application menu to open the **Mockup** panel.

The **Mockup** panel contains several categorized photographs from Adobe Stock that are perfect for branding and product placement. When the panel is open and a Mockup object is selected, you can view a preview of the full composition in the **Mockup** panel.

6. Hover your cursor across any of the previews from this panel to reveal a set of options, including **Edit On Canvas** and **License** (to license the photograph from Adobe Stock).

If you choose **Edit On Canvas** without a license for that image, a low-resolution, watermarked preview will be used.

Panoramic Virtual Reality Animations with Adobe Animate

Although we explored virtual reality (VR) using Adobe Animate in Chapter 8, we focused on creating an interactive VR 360 project with no animation. Let's take another look at VR in Animate, but this time, let's focus on a VR panoramic project with the addition of animated content.

NOTE You can create animated content in the same way as you see here using VR 360 documents. In Chapter 8, we focused on motionless, interactive VR, so it was not addressed.

The VR Panorama document type is used to wrap a panoramic image to the inside of a cylinder, which allows the user to look side to side in the experience. This differs quite a bit from the VR 360 project you created in Chapter 8, as that allows the viewer to look freely in all directions without restriction.

Another big difference between the two project types is that a VR Panorama document does not require an equirectangular image. Instead, you can use any image that is wider than it is tall, and the actual dimensions of your image do not matter as much (unlike with VR 360 images, which need to conform to a 2:1 ratio). It's much easier to create such an image using tools like Adobe Photoshop or Adobe Firefly, and you can even use the drawing tools in Animate itself to draw vector content directly in your texture layer to be used as a projection.

For this exercise, you'll be using a panoramic image file named *pano.png*, which is included in the exercise files for this chapter.

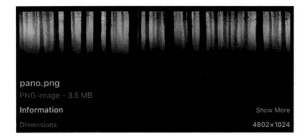

pano.png
PNG image - 3.5 MB
Information   Show More
Dimensions   4802×1024

The panoramic image you will use in this project was generated in Firefly, edited
in Photoshop, and greatly expanded in width using generative fill.

Creating and Configuring a VR Panorama Project

Let's walk through the basics.

1. From the home screen, click **Create New** in the upper left.

   The **New Document** dialog box appears.

2. From the preset categories along the top of the dialog box, click **Advanced**.

3. Scroll down to the Beta Platforms group of presets and select **VR Panorama (Beta)**.

NOTE Generative fill is
a feature in Photoshop
that leverages Firefly
generative AI to expand
an image beyond its
bounds using the Crop
tool or to add visual
content to an image
using selection tools.
Learn more about gen-
erative fill by visiting
*adobe.com/products/
photoshop/generative-
fill.html.*

NOTE As mentioned
in Chapter 8, both
VR project types in
Animate are in beta at
the time of this writing.

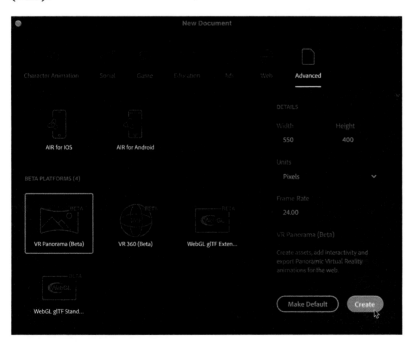

4. Click **Create** to create a new VR Panorama (Beta) document in Animate.

5. Save your document by choosing **File** > **Save** from the application menu and
   giving your new project file the name *vr.fla*.

Importing and Configuring the Content

Now that you have the proper document type created, you'll import and configure your content to work in VR space.

1. Locate the *pano.png* image and drag it onto the stage. Alternatively, choose **File** > **Import** > **Import to Stage** from the application menu to locate and import the file.

NOTE The stage in an Animate project is the rectangular canvas in the center of the application interface.

It is obvious that the imported image is much larger than the tiny stage! Let's fix that next.

2. In the **Properties** panel, choose the **Doc** tab along the top of the panel to view the document properties.

3. Click **Match Contents** under the **Document Settings** section.

   The stage width and height are adjusted to match the imported image.

4. Double-click the *Layer_1* layer name in the timeline below the stage. Rename it **Background**.

5. Hover to the right of the layer name to display toggles for the layer.

6. Click the **Create Texture Wrapping** toggle  to mark this layer for texture wrapping.

Marking a layer for texture wrapping uses the layer contents as the background projection of the immersive VR experience when published or previewed.

7. Choose **View** > **Magnification** > **Show All** from the application menu to view the entirety of the panoramic stage.

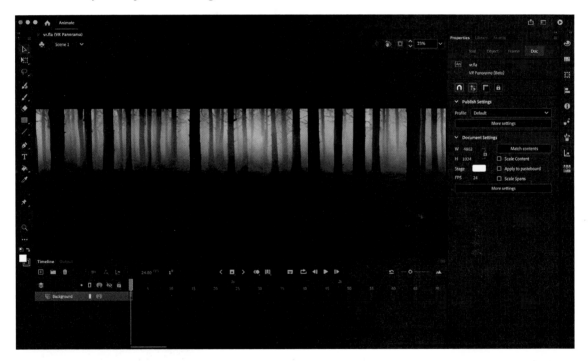

You've created a simple VR experience that, once published, will allow the viewer to drag the screen back and forth to view the entirety of the panoramic environment. Unlike with a VR 360 project, you can pan only from side to side, left or right. All other movements are locked.

Included in the files for this chapter is a version of your little ghost friend from Chapter 5. It is a PNG file named *ghost.png*.

Preparing the Timeline and Importing the Ghost

I used the Asset Export panel to export the ghost as an image asset from the Adobe Illustrator document you worked with in Chapter 5. You used the Asset Export panel in Chapter 4 to export 3D models designed in Illustrator.

1. Click the **New Layer** icon ⊞ above the existing layer to create a new layer.

2. Rename this new layer by double-clicking the layer name and entering *Ghost*.

   Animated content must exist in its own layer, and content in a texture wrapping layer can never be animated.

3. Lock the Background layer by clicking beneath the **Lock or Unlock All Layers** icon 🔒 to the right of that layer.

   Locking the Background layer ensures you do not mistakenly place the ghost in it. The keyframe located at frame 1 in the *Ghost* layer is unfilled, since it contains no assets yet.

4. Choose **File** > **Import** > **Import to Stage** from the application menu to locate and import the *ghost.png* image file.

   The ghost appears directly in the center of the stage, and the empty keyframe in the *Ghost* layer is now filled. The ghost remains selected.

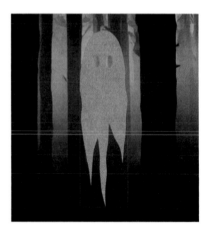

5. In the **Object** tab of the **Properties** panel, click the **Lock Width and Height Values Together** toggle  and enter the following values:

- Height: **500**
- X position: **1030**
- Y position: **230**

The ghost now appears farther in the distance and closer to the earth. You have also repositioned the ghost to the far left so it appears behind the viewer when they enter the VR experience. Spooky!

Converting the Image into a Movie Clip Symbol

You want to animate the ghost so that it playfully floats in the air among the trees. In Animate, you cannot apply animation to a bitmap image unless you first convert the bitmap into a special container called a symbol.

You will now convert the ghost bitmap image into a movie clip symbol.

1. With the ghost still selected, click the **Convert to Symbol** quick action  in the Object tab of the **Properties** panel.

The **Convert to Symbol** dialog box opens.

2. Name the symbol **LittleGhost** and choose **Movie Clip** from the **Type** menu.

3. Click **OK**.

The dialog box disappears, and your symbol is created.

The ghost bitmap image is now contained in a movie clip symbol, and a symbol instance replaces it on the stage.

The **Properties** panel changes to show that the object is now an instance of the LittleGhost movie clip symbol.

Adding Animation

With a symbol created and an instance placed on the stage where the bitmap once was, you can add a little animation to the VR project.

1. In the timeline, drag across both layers at the 2-second marker (frame 48), highlighting them.

2. From the **Insert Frames Group** control above the timeline, choose the **Frame** option to extend your frame span in both layers to frame 48.

Frames are added across both layers, and the blue playhead can now be scrubbed across 2 seconds' worth of frames.

NOTE Keyframes in Animate are somewhat like keyframes in After Effects in that they hold data values for certain properties. There are some major differences as well, as you will generally create keyframes in a more intentional way in an Animate project, depending on the type of tween you intend to use. You will use a classic tween in this section.

Notice that the only keyframes are in frame 1 of both layers. To create tweened animation, you'll need to add a few additional keyframes across the timeline.

3. Select frame 24 in the *Ghost* layer and choose **Keyframe** from the **Insert Frames Group** control above the timeline.

Clicking and holding this group reveals a menu where you can select the type of frame to insert.

4. Add an additional keyframe in the same manner at frame 48.

You now have three identical keyframes in the *Ghost* layer. You will be adjusting only properties for the ghost at the middle keyframe, keeping the first and last keyframes identical.

5. Move the playhead to frame 24, and select the ghost on the stage.

The ghost displays a rectangular blue outline, and the span of frames that represent the selected keyframe is highlighted in the timeline.

6. Choose the **Free Transform** tool  from the toolbar along the left side of the interface.

Transform handles appear around the ghost object.

7. Adjust the transform properties at frame 24 by manipulating the handles that surround the ghost to make it a bit thinner and longer, and adjust the positioning if needed.

My example resulted in a ghost that is 121 wide, 545 high, an X position of 1039, and a Y position of 224. Yours does not have to exactly match this. The idea is to provide subtle differences in the center keyframe so that the ghost appears to float in the woods. The properties of the ghost at frames 1 and 48 do not change.

8. Select any number of frames between the two frame spans on either side of the middle keyframe.

9. From the **Insert Tweens** menu above the timeline, choose **Create Classic Tween**.

A classic tween is applied to the selected frame spans. Animate will now tween any differences in properties defined across the three keyframes in the timeline.

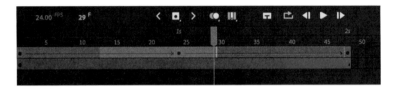

A classic tween is indicated by a black arrow that extends from one keyframe to the next. The frames that are included in the tween are violet.

10. Select any frames that make up the tween between the keyframe at frame 1 and frame 23.

11. In the **Frame** tab of the **Properties** panel, click the **Easing Effect** button in the **Tweening** section.

By default, the button is labeled **Classic Ease**.

An overlay appears that includes different ease types, easing options in each type, and an easing graph to demonstrate the form and intensity of the ease.

12. Choose **Ease Out** from the left column and select **Quad** from the options that appear.

    The graph displays the intensity curve of the chosen ease.

13. Double-click the ease to apply it to your tween and close the overlay.

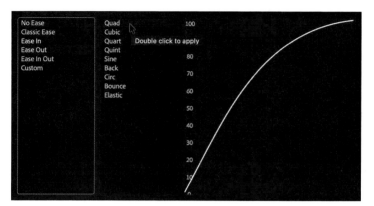

Easing creates a much more interesting and varied motion for your animation. Next, you will apply an easing effect to the send tween.

14. Select any frames that make up the tween between the keyframe at frame 24 and frame 47.

15. In the **Frame** tab of the **Properties** panel, click the **Easing Effect** button in the **Tweening** section.

    The overlay appears once more.

16. Choose **Ease In** from the left column and select **Quad** from the options that appear.

    The graph displays the intensity curve of the chosen ease.

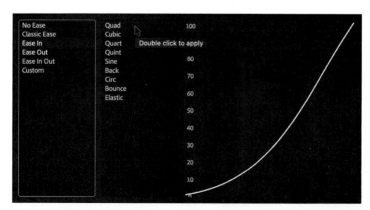

17. Double-click the ease to apply it to your tween and close the overlay.

The result of applying these easing effects on your tweens is that during the first tween, the motion begins more quickly and becomes less severe as the playhead reaches the middle keyframe. The motion will then begin slowly for the second tween and gradually become quicker as the playhead reaches 48.

This causes the ghost to appear to lift into the air slightly, hold there a bit, and then settle back to its original position.

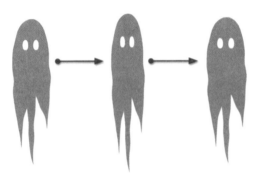

By default, the Animate project timeline will loop, causing the ghost to continue its movement the entire time the viewer is interacting with the VR experience.

Viewing the VR Project

Let's view the completed VR project in a web browser.

NOTE When you test your project in this way, Animate starts up a small local web server to get around any security issues in web browsers. You are not able to simply open the published files locally because it is a security risk. If you want to view your experience from outside Animate, you must host it on a proper web server.

1. Click the **Test Movie** icon ▶ in the upper-right corner of the interface, or choose **Control** > **Test** from the application menu.

   The project is published and opens in your default web browser.

2. Drag from side to side to view the entire experience.

   Remember, the little ghost is behind you!

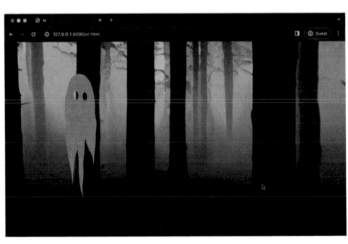

Think back to your VR 360 project from Chapter 8. How might the addition of animation flesh out the experience?

The most important thing to remember when adding interactive or animated content to any VR project in Animate is that these assets must never be placed in the texture wrapping layer. If you do place additional content in that layer, it will be rendered as part of the background projection, and animation and interactivity will not function.

NOTE For a deeper look at animation in Animate, refer to *Adobe Animate Classroom in a Book 2024 Release* (Adobe Press).

Virtual Reality with Adobe Premiere Pro

A more straightforward way of creating a VR experience is to use Adobe Premiere Pro. Since Premiere Pro is video based, you cannot include interactive elements in your production, as is possible with an Animate project. Additionally, to create a VR production, you must have access to video content that is specifically shot to be projected in virtual reality environments.

Adobe Premiere Pro uses 360° equirectangular video files to properly design your VR productions. While normal video files are projected in a rectangular perspective in front of the viewer, equirectangular videos are meant to be projected across the inside of a sphere, with the viewer at the very center.

With a rectangular image projected in front of the viewer, the viewer has a boxy, television-like experience.

When the equirectangular image is projected across the entire inner face of the sphere, the viewer is completely immersed.

NOTE VR 360 (Beta) projects in Animate use equirectangular media. Otherwise, the workflow is identical to what you have already explored. Premiere Pro works only with equirectangular content for VR.

Once the image is projected across the sphere, the viewer can look in all directions in an immersive way.

To use VR footage in Premiere Pro, it is a simple matter of including the proper video file types in your project and adding them to a sequence as you would any other media.

1. Right-click any imported video footage file in the project bin and choose **Modify** > **VR Properties** from the menu that appears.

   This reveals the Modify Clip dialog box and takes you directly to the VR Properties tab.

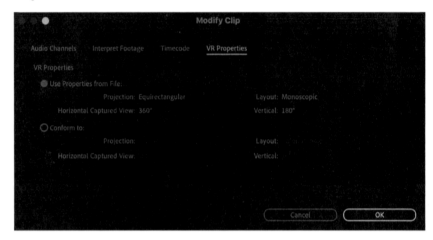

   From this dialog box, you can choose to use the VR properties embedded in the file itself or conform to specific projection and layout settings for your project. This is especially useful if Premiere Pro does not detect VR properties in your chosen file or if you need to override the embedded properties for some reason.

   You must also enable VR video in the Program Monitor to experience the projection properly.

2. Click the **Settings** button at the bottom of the Program Monitor to open the Settings menu and choose **VR Video** > **Enable** to enable the proper projection in the monitor view.

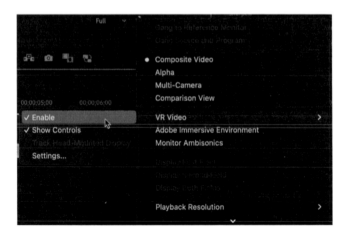

If the Show Controls option is also enabled from this same menu, a small control dial appears beneath the video, as well as perspective controls along the bottom and right of the video projection. These allow precise control over the view within your project.

NOTE To learn more about working with projects in Premiere Pro, refer to *Adobe Premiere Pro Classroom in a Book 2024 Release* which covers these video workflows.

Additionally, you will be able to drag across the view to adjust the perspective.

Good Luck!

While you've explored a lot of great software applications in this book, do not forget that other software exists—much of it outside the Adobe ecosystem.

A couple of examples that are logical additions to explore are Cinema 4D Lite, which comes bundled with Adobe After Effects, and Blender, which is open source, free, and increasingly popular. Once you are familiar with Cinema 4D Lite, you might consider exploring the full version as well. You can find more information about these tools at the following links:

- **Cineware for After Effects:**
  www.maxon.net/en/cinema-4d/features/cineware-for-after-effects

- **Blender:**
  www.blender.org

Of course, if you'd like to spend more time digging into what Substance 3D applications have to offer, you can access several tutorials on the Adobe website for free:

- **Adobe Substance 3D Tutorials:**
  https://substance3d.adobe.com/tutorials

I hope you have enjoyed exploring the exciting integrations and workflows in dedicated 3D software and their intersection with traditional 2D design software. With the concepts you have learned, you can now produce a wide variety of realistic content across still media design, interactive media, motion design, video production, and more. You have also acquired a solid foundation to build upon if you decide to explore additional 3D workflows and software. Good luck on the journey ahead!

Glossary

2D: Describes two-dimensional designs such as those traditionally created with software like Adobe Photoshop and Illustrator. Properties are measured across two dimensions: x and y.

3D: Three-dimensional design using either 2D elements in 3D space or true 3D assets. Adds a third dimension to two-dimensional design properties, most commonly in the form of a z-axis. In many applications, 2D and 3D elements can exist in the same composition or project.

AI: Adobe Illustrator project file format. The AIC file format is the cloud-based version.

AI (artificial intelligence): Describes the "intelligence" exhibited by machines and software as opposed to human intelligence. Many types of AI have been in practice for decades, though the recent surge of AI has been focused on conversational and generative AI. Adobe uses its AI (named Sensei) to perform tasks such as subject identification and image cleanup routines in Photoshop, automated lip-sync in Animate, and certain tasks across Substance 3D and mobile apps like Capture. Recently, Adobe has entered the field of generative AI with the introduction of Firefly.

API (application programming interface): Normally, a set of exposed methods and properties that developers can access to extend and augment what is available in the core application. At times, an API can be leveraged by the main developers but is most often used by a third party.

AR (augmented reality): Refers to the application of additional layers of content over real spaces. While virtual reality immerses the viewer in a fully realized environment, augmented reality overlays additional content in existing, real spaces.

Adobe: Officially "Adobe, Inc." Primarily a software development company known for professional design software such as Photoshop, Illustrator, and so on as part of the Creative Cloud subscription. They also offer a new set of 3D-focused software like the Substance 3D collection. In addition to such creative software applications, Adobe also has a hand in document management and marketing.

Aero: Primarily accessible on mobile devices (but can also be used as a beta on macOS and Windows), Adobe Aero is a tool for designing and experiencing interactive augmented reality experiences. Both 2D and 3D assets can be used when constructing an Aero experience.

After Effects: A leading visual effects, composition, animation, and motion design application that is part of Adobe Creative Cloud.

Allegorithmic: A French software company that was acquired by Adobe in 2019. All the Substance 3D applications either are derived from Allegorithmic software or were developed by what has been re-branded Substance 3D.

Anchor point: In vector design, an anchor point is any point along a path that allows control over aspects of that path through anchor point positioning or adjusting the path curvature through manipulation of anchor point handles.

Animate: Formerly known as Flash Professional, Adobe Animate is a platform-agnostic animation and interaction authoring tool that includes VR capabilities and can use 3D models through a subset of design workflows.

Behance: A social sharing network for creatives that is hosted by Adobe. Users can share their work and attend livestreams presented by other creatives.

Bitmap: Also known as a *raster image*, bitmaps are composed of pixels arranged in rows and columns along a grid. Mostly used for 2D photographic work.

CPU (central processing unit): Considered the "brain" of most computers. When dealing with 3D workflows, the CPU can be used by software for rendering and processing tasks, but a dedicated GPU is often favored.

Camera: Many software applications, including After Effects, Animate, and Substance 3D Stager, include some sort of camera that can change the view of your environment. You can control various aspects of the camera such as framing through pan and dolly controls. Some software allows the use of multiple cameras.

Capture: Adobe Capture is a mobile application for Apple iOS and Google Android that enables the capture of materials for use in other applications.

Creative Cloud: Adobe Creative Cloud is a subscription that entitles users to access traditional design software applications such as Photoshop, Illustrator, After Effects, Animate, and much more.

Creative Cloud Desktop: A desktop application that allows users to manage their Adobe Creative Cloud and Substance 3D applications.

Decal: In many Substance 3D applications, you can apply a graphic to a 3D model as a decal, which functions like a sticker across the model's surface.

Deprecated: When a feature or functionality is declared deprecated, it is often still available for use, but it has also been declared that it is going away at some point and usage of the deprecated feature is not recommended.

Depth: In 3D terminology, depth can be thought of as a companion property to the width and height of an object, with depth being the third dimension, which provides volume.

Displacement: In materials that support this property, detailed height information is determined based on the original photographic imagery and represented through the material.

Dolly: The smooth forward and backward movement associated with a camera.

Dynamic Link: Allows you to work on the same composition or project in multiple programs without having to render in between. Commonly used when rendering projects from Adobe Animate and Adobe After Effects to Adobe Media Encoder for final rendering.

Easing: In motion design, easing is the opposite of linear motion, having a more dynamic ramp-up or ramp-down in speed across time. Applying an ease to motion will often make it seem more realistic and physical in nature.

Environment: A setting or scene based on geometric properties in which 3D objects, lights, and other aspects can be arranged.

Environmental light: The overall lighting applied to a 3D scene to represent either outdoor lighting or indoor lighting. It can be thought of in a more all-encompassing, ambient way in opposition to smaller, physical lights placed in the environment.

Equirectangular: A type of photographic projection for mapping a 360° environmental exposure to a flat image. Equirectangular photographs are represented as a 2:1 ratio.

Express: Adobe Express is a web-based and mobile service that enables users to composite designs with photographic imagery, shapes, text, audio, video, and more—all through its all-in-one editor.

Extrude: Adds or removes visual depth to your object. You can often specify the depth of the extrusion and specify additional properties, like a beveled edge.

FBX: This is a more advanced 3D-object file type that can also contain animation data alongside advanced materials, cameras, and lighting. It is commonly used in gaming and mixed reality applications.

Firefly: Adobe Firefly is a generative AI set of services that exists as a standalone web experience while also integrated into software like Express, Photoshop, and Illustrator.

Fresco: The premier Adobe drawing and painting application, available primarily for tablets and other mobile devices.

GIF: A bitmap image format that is limited to 256 colors. GIF files can be animated or static. Portions of a GIF can be fully transparent or fully opaque.

GLB: GLB is a binary version of GLTF.

GPU (graphics processing unit): In 3D technologies especially, a high-powered GPU can be useful in offloading heavy, graphically focused tasks from the computer's CPU.

GTLF: This file type has capabilities like those of an FBX file but is open source (FBX is proprietary). Due to its open nature, it is often used as a 3D-file format on the web. (GLB is a binary version of GLTF.)

Gizmo: A gizmo appears as an overlay on a selected object and often exhibits different colors for each of the 3D axes you can manipulate—x, y, and z. In addition, the various shapes and spines that make up the gizmo's form represent properties such as position, scale, and rotation along each axis.

Ground plane: The floor of a 3D environment. Often, gridlines are displayed on the ground plane to provide perspective when assembling 3D objects.

HDRi (high dynamic range imagery): HDRi files can be used to determine environmental lighting in software like Substance 3D Stager and Adobe After Effects.

Illustrator: The premier Adobe vector graphics design software. Illustrator can transform vector paths into 3D representations that can be exported and used in 3D software.

Inflate: Gives the effect of your object puffing out as though filled with air.

JPEG (Joint Photographic Experts Group): This image file uses lossy compression to create a smaller file size than similar formats. Capable of millions of colors and often used in photography, the file extensions *.jpg* and *.jpeg* are often used interchangeably.

Keyframe: Placed at specific points along a timeline, a keyframe holds data for one or more properties of an object or layer. Keyframes are often used to produce changes in an object over time.

Light: Both physical and environmental lights are used to provide lighting and shadows to 3D objects when assembled in a scene.

Linear: A type of movement in which the velocity does not change across time. This is in opposition to movement that has easing applied to it.

MDL (Material Definition Language): This is an Adobe Standard material and a subset of the NVIDIA Material Definition Language.

MP4: MPEG-4 Part 14 is a container format often associated with the H.264 video codec (compression/decompression tool). This video format is incredibly popular and widely supported across hardware and software.

Material: At times referred to as textures, materials are representative of the appearance of real-world objects and are applied to 3D models to make them photographically realistic.

Media Encoder: Adobe Media Encoder is a utility application used to transcode audio and video files based on a set of presets or even advanced property definitions. It uses Dynamic Link to render projects directly from other Adobe software.

Mesh: Composed of polygonal shapes, a mesh combines points across x, y, and z axes to determine height, width, and depth. 3D models can be composed of one or many meshes.

Model: A 3D model is composed of one or more meshes to represent an object in 3D-design software or similar applications. Models can have materials and graphics applied to them to represent their appearance more realistically.

OBJ: A universal format for 3D geometry that can be used in any 3D-design software.

Orbit: A circular motion that moves in a path around a certain object or point. Often remains focused on a certain point.

PBR (physically based rendering): Describes the physical nature of the materials being represented so that lighting can be applied in a realistic and accurate way under any lighting condition. Considered a more accurate representation of how light interacts with material properties through shading and rendering.

PSD: The file extension for a Photoshop project file. A cloud-based Photoshop document has the extension PSDC.

Pan: Directional movement associated with a camera. Generally left and right horizontal movement but can also be vertical.

Parallax: Achieved in motion design when layers of content are set closer to or farther from the camera. The camera movement gives the appearance of certain objects moving more quickly or slowly away from one another depending on their distance and position.

Parametric filters: Photoshop filters that are applied directly to layers and use Substance 3D technologies to modify and influence photographic imagery.

Path: When dealing with vector graphics, a path is defined by the anchor points that are placed along it and the handles that emerge from those anchors.

Photoshop: Adobe Photoshop is the industry standard in raster-based graphic design and compositing. Photoshop includes many intersections with 3D technologies in the form of materials and filters.

Physical light: As opposed to a more general environmental light, physical lights are placed at specific points in 3D space and include variants such as spotlights, pin lights, area lights, parallel lights, and more. Unlike environmental lights, physical lights are treated more like objects.

Plane: A flat surface that can be manipulated in 3D space. The object retains its 2D appearance, with only the perspective changing.

Premiere Pro: Adobe Premiere Pro is a video sequencing software that includes the ability to translate and work with 360° equirectangular video files.

REAL: An Adobe Aero project file, which can be shared with other designers as a unique project or backed up locally. By default, Aero projects exist only in the cloud.

Ray tracing: A technique that shoots light rays throughout the scene, which the light bounces off, creating realistic reflections and shadows.

Rendering: The last step in many 3D workflows, rendering is a process that creates a photorealistic 2D image from 3D models or a 3D scene. Depending on the rendering engine and settings being used, it can be an intensive process.

Resolution: Determined by the width and height of a texture or image. The greater the resolution, the more detail and realism are available.

Revolve: Creates a 3D object along a circular, sweeping path, appearing as if formed on a physical lathe.

SBSAR: A Substance material as developed by Allegorithmic, the precursor to Adobe Substance 3D. These advanced materials can exhibit custom tweakable properties, a set of explicit presets, and more.

SPP: A Substance 3D Painter project file.

SSA: A Substance 3D Sampler project file.

SSG: A Substance 3D Stager project file.

Spin: Motion that adjusts the rotation of an object along one or more axes across time.

Stock: Adobe Stock is a library of assets that contains all sorts of useful content for photography, illustration, video content, and more.

Substance 3D: An ecosystem of apps and content that empowers you to design 3D content. The Adobe Substance 3D collection is a separate subscription from Adobe Creative Cloud.

Substance 3D Assets: A library of thousands of 3D assets, including models, materials, and lights, created by world-class artists for a variety of industries.

Substance 3D Community Assets: A library of 3D assets, including models, materials, and lights, created by the community.

Substance 3D Designer: Author seamless materials, patterns, image filters, and lights with an Academy Award–winning app and node-based workflow.

Substance 3D Modeler: Create 3D models using digital clay with hands-on tools that make modeling feel as gestural and natural as real-world sculpting. Available only on Windows at the time of this writing.

Substance 3D Painter: Paint detailed effects directly onto the surface of 3D models with parametric brushes and smart materials.

Substance 3D Sampler: Turn real-life pictures into 3D models, materials, or lights; then mix and blend assets to create even more advanced surfaces.

Substance 3D Stager: Assemble and render photorealistic scenes. Use premade templates built by world-class photographers for stunning results in minutes.

Texture: Often referred to as *materials*, textures are representative of the appearance of real-world objects and are applied to 3D models to make them photographically realistic.

USD (Universal Scene Description): Developed by Pixar, USD is a framework typically used to store entire scenes' data.

USDA: A non-binary subformat of USD that is human-readable.

USDZ: A subformat of USD, specifically created by Apple and Pixar for use in 3D-augmented reality applications.

UV: UV mapping involves taking a 2D image and applying it to a 3D object to completely wrap it in specific textures.

VR (virtual reality): A complete, simulated environment that is experienced through some form of computer hardware and software. All aspects of a VR environment are generated by the computer.

VR 360: A type of virtual reality application that enables the viewer to shift their gaze across the environment with full freedom of movement.

VR Panorama: A type of virtual reality application that restricts the viewer's gaze across the environment to left and right movements only.

Vector: A type of graphic that is rendered from mathematical data represented to paths and points. Infinitely scalable due it their mathematical nature, vectors are often used to construct logos, icons, and similar assets.

WebGL (Web Graphics Library): WebGL is a JavaScript API used for rendering interactive 2D graphics and 3D models in modern web browsers through the HTML Canvas element.

Wireframe: A skeletal representation of a 3D model in which only lines and vertices are displayed. Often used to view the base form of a model or in certain workflows that do not require detailed rendering.

Workspace: A workspace, in design software, is a specific arrangement of panels and tools often focused on a specific task or workflow.

XR (mixed reality): An umbrella term that encapsulates both virtual reality and augmented reality.

Index